POEMS & Songs of Old Lancashire

By EDWIN WAUGH.

PRINTWISE PUBLICATIONS LIMITED
1992

Published by Printwise Publications Ltd
47 Bradshaw Road, Tottington, Bury, Lancs, BL8 3PW.

Warehouse and Orders
40-42 Willan Industrial Estate, Vere Street,
(off Eccles New Road),
Salford, M5 2GR.
Tel: 061-745 9168
Fax: 061-737 1755

Originally published 1862
as POEMS AND SONGS

This edition based on the 1889 version by W. E. Clegg, 30 Market Place, Oldham, and Gilbert G. Walmsley, 50 Lord Street, Liverpool. Illustrations taken from above edition.

Reprint organised and additional material by

Cliff Hayes

ISBN 1 872226 27 2

Printed and bound by Manchester Free Press, Paragon Mill, Jersey Street, Manchester M4 6FP.
Tel 061-236 8822.

ABOUT THE AUTHOR

EDWIN WAUGH

(1817-1890)

EDWIN WAUGH was born in Rochdale, January 29th, 1817. His earlier education he received from his mother; then he went at the age of seven years to Greenwood's School in Drake Street, from there to the National School in High Street, and finally to Mr. John Davenport's Commercial School in Entwistle Place.

Waugh was over twelve years of age when he commenced work as an errand boy for a printer (Mr. John Walker), afterwards being apprenticed to Mr. Thomas Holden, another printer.

His apprenticeship ended about 1838, and the next six years were spent in printing offices in various parts of the country. He then returned to Rochdale, and for three years worked for his old employer, Thomas Holden. In 1847 he left the printing trade and became assistant secretary to the Lancashire Public Schools Association.

In 1852 he began literary work in earnest, and in 1856 made his name with the poem, "Come Whoam to thi Childer an' Me," which was published in the *Manchester Examiner and Times* on June 17th. At one bound Waugh found himself famous, and impelled by his unexpected success, he produced during the next two or three years his best poems in the dialect. These were collected and published in 1859. Later volumes of prose and poems were "Rambles in the Lake Country" (1861), "Rambles and Reveries" (1872), and "Chimney Corner" (1879).

In 1876 a fund was raised and a committee formed to take over his copyrights, guaranteeing him a fixed annual income. This arrangement relieved him on the commercial side of authorship and left him at liberty to pursue his various literary projects.

The last forty years of Waugh's life were more particularly connected with Manchester, rather than Rochdale. He was one of the founders of the Manchester Literary Club in 1862; was made a vice-president in 1876, and remained in that office until his death. In 1882 he was granted a Civil List Pension of £90.

When Waugh was about 60 years of age his health began to show signs of serious failure. He pined for the breezes of the hills, and moved to live at Kersal Moor, where he found the nearest approach to the kind of scenery he loved so much. But his health still deteriorated, so he moved again to New Brighton in the belief that sea bathing would help him to better health. But again this was not to be. He died there on April 30th, and before he died it is reputed that he said to his servant "Get me dressed and get me back to Manchester." He was buried at St. Paul's Church on the edge of Kersal Moor. No better resting place could have been found for him. As he said in his song, "The Moorland Breeze".

Oh, lay me down in moorland ground,
And make it my last bed,
With the heathery wilderness around
And the bonny lark o'er head;
Let fern and ling around me cling
And green moss o'er me creep;
And the sweet, wild mountain breezes sing
Above my slumbers sweet.

He lies on the edge of the moorland. The sun will shine freely on his grave and the moorland wind blows over it.

Many tributes have been paid to Edwin but my favourite is the poem written by Edith Lort Bedells after she had been introduced to his poetry. She seems to sum up his efforts so well. It starts off:

Simple Tales of simple lovers,
    Noble words 'bout nobler hearts.
Told with such melodious sweetness,
    That their echoes ne'er depart

Sings he not of mighty heroes
    Fallen in unholy strife,
But of men whose high ambition
    Is to lead an honest life.

Sons of Toil and honest labour,
    Men of iron nerves and will,
But with hearts of tenderest feeling
    For a suffering brother's ill.

Edwin Waugh

THE EDWIN WAUGH DIALECT SOCIETY

Founded in March 1938 by eleven gentlemen from the Rochdale area who met regularly at the Old Clock Face Hotel in Rochdale until the start of the Second World War. They chose this venue because this was the site of Edwin Waugh's birthplace.

During the War the meetings were suspended but in October 1950 the Society was revived and has gone from strength to strength.

Following the demolition of the 'Old Clock Face' Hotel to build a new market the Society now meets at St. Andrew's United Reformed Church in Smith Street in the centre of Rochdale.

Meetings are held from October to April in the Church at 7.30pm on the 2nd Wednesday of each month and all are welcome.

Further details can be obtained from the President

Jack Lye,
1 Heights Close,
Rochdale.
OL12 6ZZ.

This book is reproduced from a 1889 edition of this lovely collectors' book. I'm sure the beauty of the words and the strength of the verse far outweigh any slight blemishes on a few of the pages, to keep the style of the reprint authentic.

INTRODUCTION

Lancashire has its wealth of good authors, poets and historians, and many a long discussion could be had on the merits of each of them. But I think it is really true to say that one of the outstanding poets of this great county EVER, must be Edwin Waugh.

Edwin Waugh seems to combine the very best of the various parts and faces of Lancashire and blend them to please almost everyone. His poetry is not the hard to read dialect lines of some, that have to be read and read over before their message or meaning comes through, but the dialect is there and you can hear the rough tones of a hard life coming to life as you read.

His work has been described as "Rich in lofty sentiment, patriotic in tone, breathing thoughts full of honest independence and warm with sympathy for the poor."

His work gives you a welcome break from the day and provokes thoughts of the great outdoors, times gone by, poorer people, and once you start reading this book you start looking forward to the next poem, the next page, the next time you can pick up and gently drift with his words. Edwin Waugh is one of the few poets that have taken the very difficult subject of the ending of our stay on this mortal coil and treated it with a humour and honesty that somehow lightens the sadness, reading his lines on passing, no-one can help but feel a little lightened, no matter how sharp the pain. My favourite being:

Owd Time — he's a troublesome codger —
Keeps nudgin' us on to decay,
And whispers, "Your nobbut a lodger:
Get ready for goin' away!"

His songs of the moorlands and nature have a wildness about them that's breathtaking, and it's true that the descriptive pieces have the reader out there with the wind in your face. It is so easy to conjure up images from Edwin's words.

Cliff Hayes

ACKNOWLEDGEMENTS

PRINTWISE PUBLICATIONS and myself are receiving an enormous amount of help and encouragement in our project of reviving what we think of as our literal heritage. May I pick out for special mention:- Tony Gibb, Charlotte St., Manchester; Alan Seddon, Browser's, Prestwich; George Kelsall, Littleborough; John Glennard, Fennel Books, Corn Exchange, Manchester; Jeff Kaye, Lymm, Cheshire; Tim, Tony and the staff at Salford Local Studies Library and Central Library, Manchester; Janet Reeder of the *Metro News*; Phil Riley of the *Salford Journal* and Guy Maylor of the *Manchester Evening News*.

CONTENTS

The Moorland Flower.

I.

BENEATH a crag, whose forehead rude
O'erfrowns the mountain side,—
Stern monarch of the solitude,
Dark-heaving, wild, and wide,—
A floweret of the moorland hill
Peeped out unto the sky,
In a mossy nook, where a limpid rill
Came tinkling blithely by.

II.

Like a star-seed, from the night-skies flung
Upon the mountains lone,
Into a gleaming floweret sprung,—
Amid the wild it shone;
And bush and brier, and rock and rill,
And every wandering wind,
In interchange of sweet good-will
And mutual love did bind.

III.

In the gloaming grey, at close of day,
Beneath the deepening blue,
It lifted up its little cup,
To catch the evening dew:
The rippling fall, the moorfowl's call,
The wandering night-wind's moan;
It heard, it felt, it loved them all,—
That floweret sweet and lone.

IV.

The green fern wove a screening grove
  From noontide's fervid ray;
The pearly mist of the brooklet kist
  Its leaves with cooling spray;
And when dark tempests swept the waste,
  And north winds whistled wild,
The brave old rock kept off the shock,
  As a mother shields her child.

V.

And when it died, the south wind sighed,
  The drooping fern looked dim;
The old crag moaned, the lone ash groaned,
  The wild heath sang a hymn;
The leaves crept near, though fallen and sere,
  Like old friends mustering round;
And a dew-drop fell from the heather-bell
  Upon its burial ground.

VI.

For it had bloomed content to bless
  Each thing that round it grew;
And on its native wilderness
  Its store of sweetness strew:
Fair link in nature's chain of love,
  To noisy fame unknown,
There is a register above,
  E'en when a flower is gone.

VII.

So, lovingly embrace thy lot,
  Though lowly it may be,
And beautify the little spot
  Where God hath planted thee:
To win the world's approving eyes
  Make thou no foolish haste,—
Heaven loves the heart that lives and dies
  To bless its neighbouring waste.

The World.

I.

THIS foolish world doth wink
Its cunning lid;
And when it thinks, it thinks
Its thoughts are hid.

II.

Its piety's a screen
Where vice doth hide;
Its purity's unclean;
Its meekness, pride.

III.

Its charity's a bait
To catch a name;
Its kindness covers hate;
Its praise is blame.

IV.

Its wisdom soweth seeds
Which follies prove;
And its repentance needs
Repenting of.

V.

Its learning's empty talk;
Its heart is cold;
Its church is an exchange;
Its god is gold.

VI.

Its pleasures all are blind,
  And lead to pain ;
Its treasures are a kind
  Of losing gain.

VII.

Lust moves it more than love,
  Fear more than shame ;
Its best ambitions have
  A grovelling aim.

VIII.

Its laws are a disgrace ;
  Its lords are slaves ;
Its honours are misplaced,
  E'en on our graves.

IX.

Some sorrow doth attend
  Its happiest dreams ;
And rottenness doth end
  Its rotten schemes.

X.

Oh, cure this moral madness,—
  This soul-disease ;
Shew us that Vice brings sadness,
  And Virtue, ease :

XI.

And teach us in the hour
  Of Sin's dismay,
That Truth's the only flower
  Without decay.

Keen Blows the North Wind.

I.

KEEN blows the north wind; the woodlands are bare;
The snow-shroud lies white on the flowerless lea;
The red-breast is wailing the death of the year,
As he cowers his wing in the frozen haw-tree.

II.

The leaves of the forest, now summer is o'er,
Lie softly asleep in the lap of decay.
And the wildflower rests on the snow-covered shore,
Till the cold night of winter has wandered away.

III.

Oh, where are the small birds that sang in yon bowers
When last summer smiled on the green-mantled plain?
Oh, where do they shelter in winter's bleak hours?
Will they come back with spring, to delight me again?

IV.

But I may be gone, never more to behold
The wildflowers peep, when the winter has fled;
The chill drifts of sorrow the wanderer may fold,
And the sunshine of spring melt the snow on his bed.

V.

But come, ye sweet warblers, and sport in the spray,
  Whose tender revival I never may see;
The young buds will leap to your welcoming lay,—
  'Twill cheer the sad-hearted, as oft it cheered me.

VI.

And should ye, returning, then find me at rest,
  Stay sometimes, and sing near the grave of a friend;
Drop a rosemary leaf on his turf-covered breast,
  And rejoice that his troublesome journey's at end.

The Captain's Friends.

I.

I WANDERED down by yonder park one quiet autumn day,
When many a humble traveller was going on the way;
And there I saw a company of neighbours great and small,
All gathered round an ancient gate that leads unto the hall.

II.

The faded leaves that rustled in the mournful autumn wind
Awoke in me a train of thought that saddened all my mind;
And through the crowd of anxious folk there went a smothered wail,
So I sat me down upon a stone and hearkened to the tale.

III.

The sturdy farmer from his fields had hurried to the place,
The cripple on his crutches, and the sick with pallid face;
The poor old dame had wandered with her blind man to the ground,
And the lonely widow, weeping, with her children gathered round.

IV.

The well-remembered beggar, too, was there,—but not to beg;
And the stiff old Chelsea pensioner, upon a wooden leg:
From hamlet, fold, and lonely cot, the humble poor were there,
Each bringing in his moistened eye a tributary tear.

V.

Up spake the sturdy farmer to the porter, and he said,
"What news is this that's going round? They say the Captain's dead!"
The quaint old porter laughed, "Aha! Thank God, it isn't true!
It's but the Captain's dog that's dead,—they called it 'Captain' too!"

VI.

Then sprang the cripple on his crutch, and nearly came to ground;
The blind man wandered to and fro, and shook their hands all round;
The dame took snuff, the sick man smiled, and blest the happy day;
And the widow kissed her young ones, as she wiped their tears away.

VII.

Up rose the children's voices, mingling music with the gale,
And the beggar's dog romped with them, as he barked and wagged his tail;
The farmer slapt his thumbs, and cried, "Come on, I'll feast you all!"
And the stark old soldier with his stick kept charging at the wall.

VIII.

So, now the Captain's dog is dead and sleeping in the ground,
A kind old master by the grave bemoans his gallant hound;
He says, "My hair is white and thin! I have not long to stay!
And, oh, my poor old dog, how I shall miss thee on the way!"

IX.

Then here's to every noble heart that's gentle, just, and
brave,
That cannot be a tyrant, and that grieves to see a slave.
God save that good old Captain long, and bring his soul
to joy;—
The countryside will lose a friend the day he comes to die.

Willy's Grave.

I.

THE wintry wind was wailing wild,
Across the moorland wold;
The cloudless vault of heaven was bright
With studs of gleaming gold;
The weary cotter's heavy lids
Had closed with closing day;
And, on his silent hearth, a tinge
Of dying fire-light lay.

II.

The ancient village seemed asleep
Beneath the starry sky;
A little river, sheathed in ice,
Came gliding gently by;
The grey church in the grave-yard,
Where "the rude forefathers lay,"
Stood, like a mother, waiting till
Her children came from play.

III.

No footsteps trod the tiny town;
The drowsy street was still;
Save where the wandering night-wind sang
Its requiem wild and shrill:
The stainless snow lay thick upon
Those quaint old cottage eaves;
And wreathes of fairy frost-work hung
Where grew last summer's leaves.

IV.

Each village home was dark and still,
  And closed was every door;
For gentle sleep had twined her arms
  Around both rich and poor,—
Save in one little cot, where, by
  A candle's flickering ray
A childless mother sighing sat,
  And combed her locks of grey.

V.

Her husband, and her children all,
  Were in the silent bed,
Where, one by one, she'd laid them down,—
  And left them with the dead;
Then, toiling on towards her rest,—
  A lonely pilgrim, she,—
For God and poverty were, now,
  Her only company.

VI.

Upon the shady window-sill,
  A well-worn bible lay;
Against the wall a coat had hung,
  For many a weary day;
And, on the scanty table-top,
  With crumbs of supper strewn,
There stood, beside a porringer,
  Two little empty shoon.

VII.

The fire was waning in the grate;
  The spinning-wheel at rest;
The cricket's song rang loudly in
  That lonely woman's nest;
As, with a napkin, thin, and worn,
  And wet with many a tear,
She wiped the little pair of shoon
  Her darling used to wear.

VIII.

Her widowed heart had often leaped
  To hear his prattle small;
He was the last that she had left,—
  The dearest of them all;
And, as she rocked her to and fro,
  While tears came dreeping down,
She sighed, and cried, "Oh, Willy, love,—
  These little empty shoon!"

IX.

With gentle hand she laid them by,—
  She laid them by with care;
For, Willy, he was in his grave,—
  And all her thoughts were there:
She paused before she dropped the sneck,
  That closed her lambless fold,—
It grieved her heart to bar the door,
  And leave him in the cold.

X.

A thread-bare cloak she lapped around
  Her limbs, so thin and chill;
She left her lonely cot behind,
  While all the world was still;
And through the solitary night,
  She took her silent way,
With weeping eyes, towards the spot
  Where little Willy lay.

XI.

The pallid moon had climbed aloft
  Into the welkin blue;
A snow-clad tree across the grave
  Its leafless shadow threw;
And, as that mournful mother sat
  Upon a mound thereby,
The bitter wind of winter sighed
  To hear her lonely cry!

XII.

My little Willy's cowd an' still,—
  He's not a cheep for me!
Th' last tremblin' leaf has dropt away
  Fro' this poor withered tree!
God help my heart! my comfort's gone!
  I 'm lonely under th' sky!
He 'll never clip my neck again,
  An' tell me not to cry!

XIII.

My darlin' lad! He's laid i'th dust!
  My little Willy's dead!
An' all that made me cling to life,
  Lies in his frosty bed!
He 's gone! He 's gone! My poor bare nest!
  Oh, what's this world to me!
My little love! I'm lonely now!
  When mun I come to thee!

XIV.

He's crept into his last dark nook,
  And left me pinin' here!
An' never-moor his two blue e'en
  For me mun twinkle clear!
He 'll never say his prayers again
  At his poor mammy's knee!
Oh, Willy, love! I'm lonely now;
  When mun I come to thee!

XV.

The snow-clad yew-tree stirred with pain
  To hear that plaintive cry;
The old church listened; and the spire
  Kept pointing to the sky;
With kindlier touch, the frosty wind
  Played in her locks of grey;
And the queenly moon, upon her head,
  Shone with a softened ray.

XVI.

She rose to leave that lonely bed;
  Her heart was grieving sore;
One step she took, and then, her tears
  Fell faster than before:
She turned and gave another look,—
  One lingering look she gave,—
Then, sighing, left him lying in
  His little wintry grave.

Time is Flying.

I.

TIME is flying!
Are we hieing
To a brighter, better bourne?
Or, unthinking,
Daily sinking
Into night that knows not morn?

II.

Oh, what is life
But duty's strife?
A drill; a watchful sentry's round;
A brief campaign
For deathless gain;
A bivouac on battle ground:

III.

An arrow's flight;
A taper's light;
A fitful day of sun and cloud;
A flower; a shade;
A journey made
Between a cradle and a shroud.

IV.

Oh, what is death?
A swordless sheath;
A jubilee; a mother's call;
A kindly breast,
That offers rest
Unto the poorest of us all;

V.

The wretched's friend;
Oppression's end;
The outcast's shelter from the cold;
To regions dim,
The portal grim
Where misers leave their loads of gold;

VI.

A voyage o'er;—
A misty shore,
With time-wrecked generations strown;
Where each mad age
Has spent its rage
Upon a continent unknown.

The Moorlands.

I.

SING, hey for the moorlands, wild, lonely, and stern,
Where the moss creepeth softly all under the fern ;
Where the heather-flower sweetens the lone highland lea,
And the mountain winds whistle so fresh and so free !
I've wandered o'er landscapes embroidered with flowers,
The richest, the rarest, in greenest of bowers,
Where the throstle's sweet vesper, at summer day's close,
Shook the coronel dews on the rim of the rose ;
But, oh for the hills where the heather-cock springs
From his nest in the bracken, with dew on his wings !
Sing, hey for the moorlands !

II.

I've lingered by streamlets that water green plains,
I've mused in the sunlight of shady old lanes,
Where the mild breath of evening came sweetly and slow
From green nooks where bluebells and primroses grow;
But, oh the wild hills that look up at the skies,
Where the green bracken wave to the wind as it flies!
Sing, hey for the moorlands!

III.

Away with the pride and the fume of the town,
And give me a lodge in the heatherland brown;
Oh there, to the schemes of the city unknown,
Let me wander with freedom and nature, alone;
Where wild hawks with glee on the hurricane sail,
And the mountain crags thrill to the rush of the gale!
Sing, hey for the moorlands!

IV.

In glens which resound to the waterfall's song,
My spirit shall play the wild echoes among:
I'd climb the dark steep to my lone mountain home,
And, heartsome and poor, o'er the solitude roam:
And the keen winds that harp on the heathery lea
Should sing the grand anthem of freedom to me!
Sing, hey for the moorlands!

To the Rose-Tree on my Window Sill.

I.

DARK is the lot of him with heart so dull
By sensual appetite's unbridled sway,
As to be blind unto the beautiful
In common things that strew the common way.
Trailing the dusty elements of death,
He crawls, in his embruted blindness, proud;
To perishable ends he draws his breath;
His life, a funeral passing through a crowd;
His soul, a shrunken corpse within; his body, but a shroud.

II.

Nature! kind handmaid of the thoughtful soul,
Be thy sweet ministrations ever mine;
Thy angel-influences keep me whole,
And lead my spirit into things divine:
Holding thy lovely garment, when a child,
I walked in simple ecstasy with thee;
And now, with sadder heart, and travel-toiled,
Thou hast a sanctuary still for me,
Where oft I find repose from earthly care and misery.

III.

In cities proud, by grovelling factions torn,
Where glittering pomp and stony-eyed despair,
Murder and stealth, the lordly and the lorn,
Squalor and wealth, divide the Christian air;—
Where prowling outcasts hug with ignorant rage
Some sense of wrong that smoulders deep within;—
Where mean intrigues their furtive battles wage;

Where they are wrong that lose, and they are right that win,—
And drowning virtue struggles with the waves of sin;—

IV.

Where drooping penitence, and pious pride;
The sons of labour and the beasts of prey;
The spoilers and the spoiled, are side by side,
Jostling unkindly on the crowded way;—
E'en there sweet Nature sings her heaven-taught songs,—
Unheeded minstrel of the fuming street,—
For ever wooing its discordant throngs
With sounds and shapes that teem with lessons meet,—
Like thee, fair rose-tree, on my window blooming sweet.

V.

Oh, floral comrade of my lonely hours,
Sweet soother of my saddest mood,
The summer's glow, the scents of summer flowers,
Are filling all my solitude:
The thick-leaved groves, whose sylvan rooflets ring
With blending lyrics poured from every tree,
The sleepy streams where swallows dip the wing,
The wild flowers, nodding in the wind, I see,—
And hear the murmurous music of the roving bee.

VI.

Taking my willing fancy by the hand,
Thou leadest me through nature like a child,
Where rustling forests robe the pleasant land,
And lonely streamlets ripple through the wild;—
Through verdant nooks, where, on the long, cool grass
The lingering dews light up the leafy shade,
In dreamy bliss, my wandering footsteps pass,
Sweeping from many a lush and bending blade
The load of liquid pearls that such a twinkling made.

VII.

Now, through a sunny glade, away, away,—
Oh, let me wander thus a while with thee,—
By many a pleasant streamlet we will play,
And gad o'er many a field in careless glee:
Thus gently, thou, when on life's pathway rude
My heart grows faint as gloomy shadows lower,
Leadest me back into a happier mood,
By some sweet, secret, heaven-inspiréd power,
That lurks in thy fringed leaf and orient-tinted flower.

VIII.

My spirit burst its prison-house of care,
And dreamily, with lingering feet, I stray
Where garden odours fill the golden air,
And blossoms tremble to the wild birds' lay;—
O'er cool moist slopes, beneath the woodland shade,
Where the blithe throstle in his chamber sings,
Then wonders at the music he has made;—
Where the lush bluebell's little censer swings,
And pleasant incense to the wandering breezes flings.

IX.

Upon a shady bank, as I recline,
Gazing, with silent joy, the landscape o'er,
I feel its varied glories doubly mine,—
My heart's inheritance, my fancy's store;
Above me waves a roof of green and gold,—
Delightful shelter from the noontide heat;
Beyond, a wandering streamlet I behold,
Where wind and sunlight on the waters meet
In silvery shimmerings, past description sweet.

X.

I hear the skylark, poised on trembling wings,
Teaching the heavenly quire his thrilling lay,
All nature seems to listen as he sings,
Hushed into stillness by his minstrelsy;—

As the blithe lyric streams upon the lea,
  Steeping the wild flowers in melodious rain,
The very dewdrops, dancing to the glee,
  Look up with me, but, like me, look in vain
To find the heaven-hid singer of that matchless strain.

XI.

Now, on rough byways, sauntering through the sun,
  From fertile haunts of man I gladly stray,
Up to the sweet brown moorlands, bleak and dun,
  While rindling waters tinkle o'er my way;
Where the free eagle lords it in the sky;
  Where red grouse, springing from the heath'ry steep,
Wake the wild echoes with their lonely cry;
  And whistling breezes unrestrainéd sweep
O'er the old hills, that in the sunlight seem asleep.

XII.

O'er yon wild height, between the rugged steeps,
  From crag to crag, in many an airy bound
Of mighty glee, the mountain torrent leaps,
  And the lone ravine trembles to the sound:
Through cave and cleft, along the narrow glen,
  The rushing thunders rage, and roll afar,
Like untamed lions struggling in their den,—
  With unavailing rage,—each rocky scar
Hurls back the prisoned roar of elemental war.

XIII.

As homeward, down a winding path I stray,
  Where mazy midges in the twilight throng
In plaintive fits of liquid melody,
  I hear the lonely ousel's vesper-song;
Odours of unseen flowers the air pervade;
  As I sit listening on a wayside mound,

Watching the daylight and its business fade,
The evening stillness fills with weird sound,
And distant waters sing their ancient choral round.

XIV.

Mild evening brings the gauzy fringe of dreams
That trails upon the golden skirts of day;
And here and there a cottage candle gleams
With cheerful twinkle o'er my drowsy way;
As flaxen-headed elves, from rambles wild,
With straggling footsteps, to their mothers hie
With woodland trophies, and with garments soiled,
All tired and pleased,—they know not, care not why;—
So from my wand'rings I return, as daylight quits the sky.

XV.

Oh, flowery leader of these fancy flights,
Epitome of Nature's charms to me,
Filling my spirit with such fine delights
As I can never more repay to thee,—
For my behoof thou donn'st the summer's sheen,
Smiling benignly on thy prison-spot,
Though exiled from that native nook of green
Where playmate zephyrs seek through bower and grot,
Through all the summer roses seek, but find thee not.

XVI.

Fair lamp of beauty, in my cloistral shade,
Though brief at best the time thou hast to shine,
By an almighty artist thou wert made,
And touched with light eternally divine.
Like a caged bird, in this seclusion dim,—
Where slanting sunbeams seldom find a way,—
Singing with patient joy a silent hymn,
That wafts my thought from worldly care away
Into the realms of Nature's endless holiday.

XVII.

Sweet specimen of Nature's mystic skill,
  Dost thou know aught of human joys and woes?
Can'st thou be gladdened by the glad heart's thrill,
  Or feel the writhing spirit's silent throes?
To me thou art a messenger of love,—
  A leaf of peace amid the storms of woe,—
Dropt in my path by that celestial Dove
  Who made all things in heaven and earth below,
That wandering man the beautiful and true might know.

Christmas Carol.

I.

LONG time ago, in Palestine,
   Upon a wintry morn.
All in a lowly cattle shed,
The Prince of Peace was born.

II.

The clouds fled from the gloomy sky;
  The winds in silence lay;
And the stars shone bright, with strange delight,
  To welcome in that day.

III.

His parents they were simple folk,
  And simple lives they led;
And in the ways of righteousness
  This little Child was bred.

IV.

In gentle thought, and gentle deed,
His early days went by;
And the light His youthful steps did lead
Came down from heaven on high.

V.

He was the friend of all the poor
That wander here below;
It was His only joy on earth
To ease them of their woe.

VI.

In pain He trod His holy path,
By sorrow sorely tried;
It was for all mankind He lived,
And for mankind He died.

VII.

Like Him, let us be just and pure,
Like Him, be true alway;
That we may find the peace of mind
That never fades away.

Now Summer's Sunlight Glowing.

I.

NOW, summer's sunlight, glowing,
  Streaks the woodland shade with gold;
And balmy winds are blowing
  Softly o'er the moorland-wold;
Now sweet smells the bluebell,
  'Neath the valley's leafy screen;
And thick grows the wild rose,
  Clust'ring o'er the hedges green.

The fern adorns the moorland steep;
  The smiling fields are flowered o'er;
And modest little daisies peep
  Like children at a mother's door!

II.

From dewy meadows springing,
  Yonder blinding skies among,
The poet-lark is singing,
  As if his heart was made of song!
While gladly and madly
  In every grove the wild birds vie,
All tingling and mingling
  In tipsy routs of lyric joy!
My throbbing heart with every part
  Is dancing to the chorus near,—
The gush, the thrill,—the wizard trill,—
  Like drops of water tinkling clear!

III.

The cottage matron, knitting
  In her little garden, sings,
As wild birds, round her flitting,
  Fan the blossom with their wings;
And twining, combining,
  The honeysuckle and the rose,
Sweet shading, and braiding,
  Round her winking lattice goes;
And wild bees through the flowers roam—
  The little happy buzzing thieves!—
Here and there, with busy hum,
  Rifling all the honeyed leaves.

IV.

Now, hamlet urchins roaming,
  All the sunny summer day,
From dewy morn till gloaming,
  Through the rustling wildwood stray;
There blithely and lithely,
  By warbling brook and sylvan grot,
They ramble and gambol,
  All the busy world forgot;—
Like birds that wing the sunny air,
  And warble in the tangled wild,
Unhaunted by the dreams of care,—
  Oh, to be again a child!

V.

Sweet scents and sunshine blending ;
The wildwoods, in their leafy pride,
To the gentle south wind bending ;—
Oh, the bonny summer tide !
The tinkling, the twinkling,
Where little limpid rivers lave ;
The sipping, the dipping
Of wild-flowers in the gilded wave ;—
The fruitful leas, the blooming trees,
The pleasant fields, embroidered fair ;
The wild birds' little melodies,
Scattering gladness everywhere !

Sea Weeds.

I.

THE land has its gardens of roses,
Its flowers of every hue,
Which close as the daylight closes,
And wake to the morning dew;
It has sweet scented groves of pleasure,
Where the bee roves all day long,
And, at eve, with her load of treasure,
Flies home to a drowsy song.

II.

There, summer her mantle of verdure,
With posies so sweet enweaves,
That the sunshine delays on their beauty,
Till it falls asleep in the leaves;
And the spell-bound rain comes dreeping,
To brighten their eyes anew;
And their folds are by young winds fondled,
And kist by the silvery dew.

III.

But the grand old sea hides wonders
That never met mortal eye,—
Bright bowers that never have rustled
To soft wind's dreamy sigh;
Strange groves of mystical beauty,
And flowers of rainbow hue.
Bloom wild in those old sea-gardens,
All under the waters blue!

IV.

And when the pale moon is sleeping,
  At night on the trembling sea,
And the coral-paved halls of Neptune
  Re-echo the kelpies' glee:
Oh, the floral festoons of magic,
  That curtain those pearly caves,
Where the water-sprites revel in splendour,
  All under the drowsy waves!

V.

Ye fairy-tinged groves of ocean,—
  Your delicate banners wave,
Where the fisherman sleeps in the lonely deeps,
  In his cold uncrowded grave:
Wave on your beautiful tendrils,
  In your gardens wild and free,
Caressed by the gleaming waters,
  Of the grand old heaving sea!

Things Gone By.

I.

'TWAS evening; sad November's gale
Was moaning wild and cold;
Night's deep'ning shade had dimm'd the vale,
And hid the distant wold;
In dreamy mood, as all grew still
Beneath the waning sky,
I sat beside my window-sill,
And thought of things gone by.

II.

An old and lonely man was there,
By labour sorely worn;
The frost of age had thinn'd his hair,
And sorrow made him lorn;
His wrinkled cheek long time had play'd
With wind, and rain, and sun;
That weary man, he sigh'd, and said—
"It's dark—and nothing done."

III.

On life, and death, and mortal fret,
I musing then began;
And on the dangers that beset
The pilgrimage of man:
I thought of days for ever flown,

And hopes for ever fled;
I sigh'd for friends asunder thrown,
Or sleeping with the dead.

IV.

Since life's first wand'ring step began
They've strewn the fatal way,
And only here and there a man
Has reach'd the close of day;
Like leaflets, drifted to and fro,
When autumn's cold winds rave,
Some fluttering wild, some trampled low,
Some mould'ring in the grave.

V.

The days are gone when light and free,
I roved the mountains wild;
The light no more will shine for me
On morning's hour that smiled:
No sun or rain can e'er again
Revive youth's faded flowers;
No sad regret, nor sigh of pain,
Recall the fleeted hours.

To a Married Lady.

I.

AH, this wild voyage o'er the sea of life
Needs all the help that heaven to earth can give;
Through its dark storms, and shoals, and battle-strife,
God must be pilot to the ships that live.

II.

Happy the heart that finds a haven of love,
Where in the tempest it can sweetly moor,
And taste, below, the bliss that but above,
Is ever stainless, and is ever sure.

III.

And blest the hearth where pure affections glow—
The husband's and the father's best retreat;
Where heavenward souls in one direction grow,
With darling tendrils round them twining sweet.

IV.

Such be thy home; through earth's mutations strange,
A garden, where the flowers of heaven grow;
And, sheltered there from blight, through every change,
Its loves, its hopes, no touch of ruin know.

V.

May Time, whose withering finger ever brings.
To Nature's best the doom of sure decline,
Float over thee with gently-fanning wings,
And find the twilight of thy life divine.

VI.

And, ever hand in hand, along your path,—
For thee and thine thus doth the poet pray,—
That ye may walk in joy from life to death,
And earth's night be the dawn of heaven's day.

Cultivate Your Men.

I.

TILL as ye ought your barren lands,
And drain your moss and fen ;
Give honest work to willing hands,
And food to hungry men ;
And hearken—all that have an ear—
To this unhappy cry,—
" Are poor folks' only chances here
To beg, or thieve, or die ? "

II.

With kindly guerdon this green earth
Rewards the tiller's care,
And to the wakening hand gives forth
The bounty slumbering there ;
But there's another, nobler field
Big with immortal gain,—
The morasses of mind untilled ;—
Go,—cultivate your men !

III.

Oh, ponder well, ye pompous men,
With Mammon-blinded eyes,
What means the poverty and pain
That moaning round you lies :
Go, plough the wastes of human mind
Where weedy ignorance grows,—
The baleful deserts of mankind
Would blossom like the rose.

IV.

But penny-wise, pound-foolish thrift
  Deludes this venal age;
Blind self's the all-engrossing drift,
  And pelf, the sovereign rage.
E'en in the Church the lamp grows dim,
  That ought to light to heaven,
And that which fed its holy flame,
  To low ambition's given.

V.

Just retribution hovers near
  This play of pride and tears;
To heaven all worldly cant is clear,
  Whatever cloak it wears;
And high and low are on one path,
  Which leads unto the grave,—
Where false distinctions flit from death,
  And tyrant blends with slave.

Old Man's Song.

I.

OH! sweetly the morning of childhood
Awoke me to careless delight;
And blithe as a bird of the wildwood
I played in its beautiful light;
The world was a magical treasure
That filled me with wonder and joy;
And I fluttered from pleasure to pleasure,
Delighted—I couldn't tell why:
If I thought of to-morrow,
I dreamt not of sorrow;
And I smiled as the day went by.

II.

Gay youth, with its glittering hours,
Came frolicking on, full of glee,
Where hope's charming sunlighted bowers
Were thickly in blossom for me;—
My heart was an harp whose emotion
Awoke to all beautiful things,
And love was the dearest devotion
That played in its tremulous strings:
So, I dallied, delighted,
And carelessly slighted
Old Time and his rustling wings.

III.

Now, the noontide of life has gone by me,
The visions of morning have died;
And the world is beginning to try me
With struggles that chasten my pride;—
As the twilight of time, softly stealing,
Comes o'er me with shadows of grey,
I feel the sad truth now revealing,—
It draws to the close of the day;
And thoughtfully eyeing
The past, I sit sighing,
And wondering how long I shall stay.

Bide On.

I.

WHEN thy heart 'neath its trouble sinks down,
And the joys that misled it are gone,—
When the hopes that inspired it are flown,
And it gropes in thick darkness, alone,—
Let faith be thy cheer,
Scorn the whispers of fear,
Be righteous, and bravely bide on.

II.

When fancy's wild meteor-ray
Allures thee from duty to roam,
Beware its bewildering way,
And rest with thy conscience at home;—
Give ear to its voice;
Let the stream of thy joys
From the fountain of purity come.

III.

When, by failure and folly borne down,
The future looks hopelessly drear;
And each day, as it flies, with a frown,
Tells how helpless, how abject we are;
Let nothing dismay
Thy bold effort to-day;—
Be patient, and still persevere.

IV.

Be steady, in joy and in sorrow;
Be truthful, in great and in small;
Fear nothing but sin, and each morrow
Heaven's blessing upon thee shall fall:
In thy worst tribulation
Shun low consolation,
And trust in the God that sees all.

The Moorland Witch.

I.

THERE lives a lass on yonder moor,—
She wears a gown of green;
She's handsome, young, and sprightly,
With a pair of roguish een:
She's graceful as the mountain doe
That snuffs the forest air;
And she brings the smell of the heather-bell
In the tresses of her hair.

II.

'Twas roaming careless o'er the hills,
As sunlight left the sky,
That first I met this moorland maiden
Bringing home her kye:
Her native grace, her lovely face,
The pride of art outshone;—
I wondered that so sweet a flower
Should blossom thus alone.

III.

Alas, that ever I should meet
  Those beaming eyes of blue,
That round about my thoughtless heart
  Their strong enchantment threw.
I could not dream that falsehood lurked
  In such an angel smile;
I could not fly the fate that lured
  With such a lovely wile.

IV.

And when she comes into the vale,
  To try her beauty's power,
She'll leave a spell on many a heart
  That fluttered free before.
But, oh, beware her witching smile,—
  'Tis but a fowler's snare;
She's fickle as the mountain wind
  That frolics with her hair!

The Church Clock.

I.

OH, thou who dost these pointers see,
And hear'st the chiming hour,
Say, do I tell the time to thee,
And tell thee nothing more ;—
I bid thee mark life's little day
By strokes of duty done ;—
A clock may stop at any time,
But time will travel on.

II.

I am a preacher to a few,—
A servant unto all,
As here I stand tick, ticking,
Like a death-watch in a wall ;
And, it were well that those who see
These fingers gliding on,
Should think a moment, now and then,
How fast the moments run.

III.

There's some of you are wealthy,
  And some of you are proud;
And some are poor, and some are sad,
  And waiting for a shroud;—
Be patient yet a while, for see
  This little yard below,—
The man who goes the longest way,
  Has not so far to go.

IV.

A christ'ning; then, a wedding comes;
  And then, a passing bell;
'Tis just the ancient tale that time
  Has always had to tell:
The very clock that marks the hour,
  With ticking wears away;
The gladdest pulse of life contains
  The music of decay.

Christmas Song.

I.

IN the dark-clouded sky no star shews a gleam;
    The drift-laden gale whistles wild in the tree;
  The ice-mantle creeps o'er the murmuring stream,
  That glittering runs through the snow-covered lea;
But, hark! the old bells fling the news to the wind!—
  Good Christians awake to their genial call;
The gale may blow on, we'll be merry and kind;
  Blithe yule, and a happy new year to us all!
    Bring in the green holly, the box, and the yew,

The fir, and the laurel, all sparkling with rime;
Hang up to the ceiling the mistletoe-bough,
And let us be jolly another yule-time!

II.

While, garnished with plenty, together we meet
In carolling joy, as the glad moments flee,
Thus sheltered away from the frost and the sleet,
With friends all around us, in festival glee,
We'll still keep the heavenly lesson in mind,—
The gentle Redeemer was born at this tide;
The wind may blow keenly, but we will be kind,
And think of the poor folk that shiver outside.
Bring in the green holly, the box, and the yew,
The fir, and the laurel, all sparkling with rime;
Hang up to the ceiling the mistletoe-bough,
And let us be jolly another yule-time!

III.

He's a cur who can bask in the fire's cheery light,
And hearken, unheeded, the winter wind blow,
And care not a straw for the comfortless wight
Who wanders about in the frost and the snow;
But we'll think of the mournful the while we are glad;
Our hearts shall be kind as the winter is keen;
And we'll share our good cheer with the poor and the sad,
Who sorrow and struggle in corners unseen.
Bring in the green holly, the box, and the yew,
The fir, and the laurel, all sparkling with rime;
Hang up to the ceiling the mistletoe-bough,
And let us be jolly another yule-time!

Love and Gold.

I.

WE were but poor young people,
My Margaret and I;
And well I knew she loved me,
Although her looks were shy:
But I longed to see strange countries,
That lie beyond the main;
And when I'd gathered riches,
Come flaunting home again.

II.

When I parted from my true love,
A rover's fate to try,
She was full of strange forebodings,
And tears were in her eye.
Pale looks of silent sorrow
She gave to all my glee,
When I said, "I'll win some gold, love,
And bring it back to thee!"

III.

But my heart was proudly beating,
And I was in my prime,
So, in chase of golden treasure,
I went from clime to clime;
In giddy chase of pleasure,
Beyond the foaming sea,
All heedless of the maiden
Who pined at home for me.

IV.

So I sought for gold, and won it,
And still I wanted more,
And as my treasure gathered,
Was poorer than before:
For it made me proud and heartless;
It made me hard and cold;
It made me slight my true love,—
That cursèd yellow gold!

V.

But, in spite of all my riches,
I was growing old and worn;
So I took a ship for England,
The place where I was born;
I took a ship for England,
With all my golden store,
To dazzle those that knew me
Full thirty years before.

VI.

When I landed with my gold-bags,
The friends of old were gone;
And, in spite of all my riches,
I felt myself alone.
Though strangers fluttered round me
I knew their hearts were cold;
And I sought in vain the true love,
That's never bought with gold.

VII.

My skin was parched and yellow,
My hair was thin and grey,
And she that loved me dearly,
Was sleeping in the clay.
She had long been in the churchyard,
Sleeping sweet and sound;
And I was but an outcast
Upon the lonely ground.

VIII.

Now to her grave I wander,
  And sit upon the stone,
Where all is still and silent,—
  Except my bitter moan:
But I shall soon be going,
  For I am ill and old;
And my gold will deck the mourners,
  Who wish my body cold.

Mountaineer's Song.

I.

COME, all you lads that wander free
  Upon the mountains wild;
That love sweet nature's liberty,
  And will not be beguiled;
With you, as blithe as moorland wind,
  I'll rove by hill and glen;
Life's greatest bliss we oft shall find
  Far from the haunts of men.

CHORUS.—Then, let the winds blow high or low,
  Beneath the changeful sky;
This world so fine shall all be mine
  Until the day I die.

II.

I care not for the stately hall,
  It is no place for me;
My purse is light, my wants are small,
  My heart is fain and free;
In lowly nest I take my rest,
  And shelter from the cold;

I bend to no man's haughty crest,
  I envy no man's gold.
      CHORUS.—Then, let the winds blow.

III.

The king may wear his jewelled crown
  Upon a weary head;
The couch on which he lays him down
  May be a sleepless bed;
The massive walls of courtly halls
  May close him in with care;
In knightly towers, and guarded bowers,
  Black grief may find him there.
      CHORUS.—Then, let the winds blow.

IV.

For me o'erhead, the heavens are spread,
  With hill and dale below;
Each murmuring stream, each sunny gleam,
  And all the winds that blow;
Where'er I stray, my lonely way
  Strewn with delight I find;
My greatest wealth is rustic health,
  My bliss a peaceful mind.
      CHORUS.—Then, let the winds blow.

V.

For me, in posied mantle green,
  Glad nature decks the spring;
For me, amidst the vernal scene,
  The happy wild-birds sing;
For my delight, each lovely sight
  The changing season thrills;
For me, the wild breeze, day and night,
  Harps on the heathery hills.

CHORUS.—Then, let the winds blow high or low,
      Beneath the changeful sky;
    This world so fine shall all be mine,
      Until the day I die.

The Moorland Maid.

I.

THERE'S a limpid rindling fountain,
Yonder moorland hills among;
From the heather-breasted mountain
Tinkling drips its liquid song;
To its lonely music list'ning,
Once a maiden sat thereby;
Oh, that maiden's dark eye glist'ning,—
It will haunt me till I die.

II.

In that fragrant, wild seclusion,
With the soaring lark above,
Blooming nature's glad profusion
Listen'd to our vows of love;
Sunny skies, and flowers around us,
On my rustic darling smiled;
And the dewy twilight found us
Ling'ring still amid the wild.

III.

Oh, mild hour, when eve's lone planet
Gilds the pearls on every blade;
Angel-zephyrs came to fan it,—
Blissful hour of mystic shade;
Sweet the wild-bird's trilling vespers
Died upon the dewy lea;
But my darling's gentle whispers
Never more will fade from me.

IV.

Ah, that scene is now too sadd'ning,—-
  Saddest in its richest bloom;
Summer flowers, the wild hills gladd'ning,
  Move my heart to deeper gloom;
Birds may hail the scented blossom
  Oft on smiling hill and plain,
But the green earth's silent bosom
  Ne'er will yield my love again.

V.

Thus to meet thee, but to sever;
  Thus to love, and then to part,—
Oh, the bliss, the pain, for ever
  Mingling in my lonely heart:
Oh, those lovely glances, darting
  Modest gleams of timid glee;
Oh, the last sad hour of parting,
  'Tween my own true love and me.

VI.

Farewell to yon breezy mountain,
  Farewell to the flow'ry dell;
Farewell to the rindling fountain,
  And the lonely moorland well;
Farewell to the streamlet, purling
  Sweetly through yon silent glen;
Oh, farewell, the dark-eyed darling
  I shall never see again!

Wild and Free.

I.

I WISH I was on yonder moor,
And my good dog with me,
Through the bonny heather-flower
Wading, wild and free :
Wild and free ;
Wild and free ;
Where the moorland breezes blow.

II.

Oh, the wilderness is my delight,
Where the whirring red grouse springs,
From his heathery nest on the mountain's breast,
With the dew upon his wings :
Wild and free ;
Wild and free ;
Where the moorland breezes blow.

III.

At the gloaming hour, in grove and bower.
The throstle chants with glee ;
But the plover sings his evening hymn
To the lone waste, wild and free :
Wild and free ;
Wild and free ;
Where the moorland breezes blow.

IV.

On the heathy hills I'll take my rest,
And there my bed shall be ;
With the lady-fern above my breast,
Waving wild and free :
Wild and free ;
Wild and free ;
Where the moorland breezes blow.

Heigho for Cobblers!

I.

OF all the craftsmen in this world,
The cobbler lad for me,
With his pegs an' tacks, an' his hemp
an' wax,
An' his lapstone on his knee.
Welt it, an' pelt it;
Pelt it, an' welt it;
Sing, heigho for cobblers!

II.

The lads that patch these poor men's shoon,
I fain would have you know,
They are the friends on whom depends
What footing you must go.
Twitch it, an' stitch it;
Stitch it an' twitch it;
Sing, heigho for cobblers!

III.

Saint Crispin was a lad of wax,
And he tugged the 'tachin-end;
And he plied his awl in his good old stall,
The soles of men to mend:
Stump it, an' clink it;
Clink it, an' stump it;
Sing, heigho for cobblers!

IV.

Then, here's good luck to the old cow's hide,
  Likewise the good lapstone ;
The man whose footsteps never slide,
  Shall seldom need to moan :
      Ring it, an' ding it ;
      Ding it, an' ring it ;
    And, heigho for cobblers !

V.

The man that keeps his top-knot cool
  Will never come to harm,
If he gets a lad with a leather-brat
  To keep his poor feet warm :
      Thump it, an' stump it ;
      Stump it, an' thump it ;
    Sing, heigho for cobblers !

VI.

Good luck attend the cobbler's awl,
  His hemp, an' nails, an' tacks,—
His knife, an' last, an' blackin'-ball,
  His bristles, an' his wax !
      'Tach it, an' catch it ;
      Catch it, an' 'tach it ;
    Sing, heigho for cobblers !

VII.

And when, at last, he quits his awl,
  And lays him down to rest,
He shall sleep sound 'neath a grassy mound
  With a lapstone on his breast :
      End it, an' mend it ;
      Mend it, an' end it ;
    Sing, heigho for cobblers !

Christmas Morning.*

I.

COME all you weary wanderers,
Beneath the wintry sky;
This day forget your worldly cares,
And lay your sorrows by;
Awake, and sing;
The church bells ring;
For this is Christmas morning!

II.

With grateful hearts salute the morn,
And swell the streams of song,
That laden with great joy are borne,
The willing air along;
The tidings thrill
With right good will;
For this is Christmas morning!

III.

We 'll twine the fresh green holly wreath,
And make the yule-log glow;
And gather gaily underneath
The winking mistletoe;
All blithe and bright
By the glad fire-light;
For this is Christmas morning!

IV.

Come, sing the carols old and true,
  That mind us of good cheer,
And, like a heavenly fall of dew,
  Revive the drooping year;
    And fill us up
    A wassail-cup;
  For this is Christmas morning!

V.

To all poor souls we 'll strew the feast,
  With kindly heart, and free;
One Father owns us, and, at least,
  To-day we 'll brothers be;
    Away with pride,
    This holy tide;
  For it is Christmas morning!

VI.

So now, God bless us one and all
  With hearts and hearthstones warm;
And may He prosper great and small,
  And keep us out of harm;
    And teach us still,
    His sweet good-will,
  This merry Christmas morning!

Here's to My Native Land.

I.

HERE'S to my native land;
And here's to the heathery hills,
Where the little birds sing on the blooming boughs,
To the dancing moorland rills.

II.

There's a lonely little cot,
And it stands by a spreading tree,
Where a kind old face has looked from the door
Full many a time for me;—

III.

On the slope of a flowery dell,
And hard by a rippling brook;
And it's oh for a peep at the chimney-top,
Or a glint of the chimney-nook!

IV.

And there is a still churchyard,
Where many an old friend lies;
And I fain would sleep in my native ground
At last, when they close my eyes.

V.

When summer days were fine,
The lads of the fold and I
Have roved the moors, till the harvest moon
Has died in the morning sky.

VI.

Oh, it's sweet in the leafy woods
On a sunny summer's day;
And I wish I was helping the moorland lads
To tumble their scented hay!

VII.

Though many a pleasant nook
In many a land I've seen,
I'd wander back to my own green hills,
If the wide world lay between.

VIII.

They say there's bluer skies
Across the foaming sea:—
Each man that is born has a land of his own,
And this is the land for me!

Minnie.

I.

MY Minnie's as shy as a little wild rose,
That fills all around with delight as it blows;
Its leaves, pleasant-scented,
Unfolding, contented
To sweeten the nook where it grows.

II.

Kate flutters her wings, and a lady would be;
She's ribboned, and jewelled, and flounced to the knee;
But she's keen, and she's cold,
And she's proud of her gold,—
The dule take her ribbons for me!

III.

My Minnie's as poor as a little red-breast,
"With nought in the wide world but God and its nest;"
Yet the star of a king
Is a pitiful thing
To the jewel that grows in her breast.

IV.

Kate's handsome and bold, and she's haughty and chill;
She's a winterly smile for the heart she can kill;
And she bears off the bell
From the girls of the dell,—
With a clapper that never lies still.

V.

Though Minnie's as blithe as the skylark that springs
From its roost in the meadow, with dew on its wings—
'Tis her own little nest,
And the mate she loves best,
That gladden the song that she sings.

VI.

What care I for riches and gaudy array—
What care I to flaunt with the heartlessly gay?
If my little wild rose
Love me on to life's close,
And sweeten its troublesome way.

Life's Twilight.

I.

NOW silver threads begin to shine
Among my thinning hair;
And down the slope of life's decline
I thoughtfully repair.
The fire that once was in mine eyes
Has dimmed its fervid ray,
And every hour of life that flies,
Is stealing light away.
Oh, let me, with untroubled breast,
A while in shadow lie,
Before I lay me down to rest,
And bid the world "Good bye."

II.

With Time, that wrestler old and grim,
  I've had a gallant round;
But ah, there's little chance with him
  Who bringeth all to ground.
Although the world still rolleth on
  Its merry, motley way,
My little part of life is done,
  Except to watch the play.
Then let me, with untroubled breast,
  A while in shadow lie,
Before I lay me down to rest,
  And bid the world "Good bye."

III.

In youth, to pleasure's lightest trill,
  My heart leaped light and free;
Now, she may play what tune she will,
  It is not so with me;
For though a smile may sometimes steal
  Across my furrowed brow,
My joys are all akin, I feel,
  To contemplation now.
Then let me, with untroubled breast,
  A while in shadow lie,
Before I lay me down to rest,
  And bid the world "Good bye."

Nightfall.

I.

THE green leaves answer to the night-wind's sigh
And dew-drops winking, on the meadows lie ;
The sun's gone down
O'er the drowsy town ;
And the brooks are singing to the listening moon.

II.

The soft wind whispers on its moody way ;
The plumy woodlands in the moonlight play ;
Night's tapers gleam
In the gliding stream ;
Heaven's eyes are watching while the earth doth dream.

III.

The lovely light that dwells in woman's eyes,
Softly curtained by the fringed lids lies ;
Sleep's Lethean hand
Waves o'er the land,
And the weary toiler to his shelter hies.

IV.

Old nurse, whose lullaby can soothe them all,
Oh, hap them kindly in thy downy pall !
They've gone astray
On life's rough way ;
But, rest them ; rest them for another day.

V.

The living, sleeping in their warm beds lie;
The dead are sleeping in the churchyard, nigh;
The mild moon's beam
O'er all doth stream,
And life and death appear a mingling dream.

VI.

Decay, that in my very breath doth creep,
Thou surely art akin to this soft sleep,
That shows the way
To a bed of clay,
Whose wakeless slumbers close the mortal day.

VII.

And thus, with ceaseless roll, time's silent wave
Lands me each night upon a mimic grave,
Whose soft repose
Hints at life's close,—
Death's fleets are cruising where life's current flows.

Oh! Come Across the Fields.

I.

NOW, from dreary winter's dream awaking,
Glad nature robes herself to meet the spring;
Hark, how the blithesome birds are making
Among the trees their songs of welcoming!
Oh, come across the fields, my love,
And through the woods with me;
As nature moves toward the spring,
So moves my heart to thee, my love,
So moves my heart to thee!

II.

See, from their silent shelters sweetly peeping,
The budding wild-flowers steal with timid glee;
See the soft fresh verdure, gently creeping,
Is mantling over the delighted lea!
Then come across the fields, my love,
And through the woods with me;
As nature moves toward the spring,
So moves my heart to thee, my love,
So moves my heart to thee!

III.

Oh! listen, love; it is the throstle's carol,
In yonder elm-tree ringing loud and clear;—
"First come the buds, and then the bonny blossom—
The golden summer time will soon be here!"
Then come across the fields, my love,
And through the woods with me;
As nature moves toward the spring,
So moves my heart to thee, my love,
So moves my heart to thee!

IV.

My heart is like a flowerless wintry wild,
Where tuneless joy sits lone, with folded wing,
Until thy beauty comes, enchantress mild,
To melt the gloom, and make the flowers spring!
Oh, shine upon this longing heart,
And I thy charms will sing,
For thy sweet re-appearing
Is like another spring, my love,
Is like another spring!

God Bless Thee, Old England.

I.

GOD bless thee, old England, the home of the free;
A garden of roses, begirt by the sea!
The wild waves that fondle thy darling green shore
Shall sing thy proud story till time be no more;
And nations unborn, looking over the wave,
Shall tell of the isle of the free and the brave,
Where liberty's battle, through ages of old,
Was fought in the hearts of the just and the bold;—
Old England, the Queen of the Sea!

II.

May truth ever flourish thy children among;
And deeds that awaken the spirit of song
Inspire future bards with emotion divine,
Till earth has no anthem so noble as thine!
Green cradle of manliness, beauty, and worth!
May thy name be a watchword of joy in the earth
When I have long mouldered beneath the green sod,—
A country devoted to freedom and God;—
Old England, the Queen of the Sea!

The Victims of War.

I.

HARK! from beyond the heaving main
Wild havoc yells afar;
The kings of earth have roused again
The fiendish game of war.
Slaughter and flame,
Ruin and shame;
Ah, me! for the pranks that rulers play,
The poor must suffer, and bleed, and pay!

II.

From slaughtered babes and blazing cot,
The frantic mother flies;
And prone upon his wasted plot
The bleeding peasant lies.
Rapine and flame,
Murder and shame;
Ah, me! for the pranks of the dominant few
The millions must suffer, and sorely rue.

III.

The pilaged town, the trampling hoof,
The ruthless, slashing blade;
The murd'rous yell, the crashing roof,
The thundering cannonade.
Slaughter and flame,
Havoc and shame;
Ah, me! for the pranks that rulers play,
The poor must suffer, and bleed, and pay!

IV.

The savage rout, the hellish shout,
  That drowns the dying wail;
The matron's moan, the strong man's groan,
  The rifle's deadly hail.
    Slaughter and flame,
    Ruin and shame;
Ah, me! for the pranks that rulers play,
The poor must suffer, and bleed, and pay!

V.

Thus ever runs the gory tale
  Of dark oppression's dreams;
Thus springs anew the bitter wail
  From craft's conflicting schemes.
    Slaughter and flame,
    Murder and shame;
Ah, me! for the pranks that rulers play,
The poor must suffer, and bleed, and pay!

Twilight Carol.*

I.

AT the close of day, her melting lay
As Philomel began,
A maiden sang as she did stray,
And thus the carol ran:

II.

Oh, the daisy, and the sweet bluebell,
And the bonny celandine;
My darling's feet have touched the dell,
And made the posies fine.

III.

Soft whispering gales, on viewless wings,
Come o'er the rippling sea;
But ah, no news the west wind brings
From my true love to me.

IV.

The wild bee roves the flowery wold;
Be still, dear heart of mine;
My darling is a cup of gold
That's running o'er with wine.

V.

Sweet bird, whose tender warble fills
The ear of fading day,
Go, sing for me those liquid trills,
That fond complaining lay.

---

* Published with music, by Messrs. Hime and Addison, Manchester.

The Wounded Lark.*

WRITTEN ON THE ILLNESS OF AN EMINENT MUSICIAN.

I.

LAY low thine ear with kindly care,
And gently tread the ground;
Some mourner haunts the grassy lair;
What means this plaintive sound?

II.

Here, 'mongst his little nestlings, lies
A lark, with broken wing,
Gazing aloft into the skies,
Where once he used to sing.

III.

No more up-springing from the lawn,
To greet the brightening sky,
High-poised, 'mid rosy tints of dawn,
He'll thrill the world with joy.

IV.

No more above the sun-tipt hills
He'll fan his happy wings;
His notes have sunk to mournful trills,
And sorrow's all he sings.

* Published with music, by Messrs. Hime and Addison, Manchester.

V.

So prone lies he, whose genial power
   Once led the tuneful train ;
So fate has changed his joyous dower
   To cadences of pain.

VI.

Thus, daily, minstrel tones do creep
   In sadness, one by one,
Into the silent land, where sleep
   The voices that are gone.

The Old Bard's Welcome Home.

I.

BRING me a goblet of drink divine,
To welcome a minstrel friend of mine !
Enfranchised from the dreary crowd,
That wrapt his spirit like a shroud,
Once more he climbs the moorlands dun,
And hears his native rindles run ;
Through pleasant vales he takes his way,
Where wild-flowers with the waters play ;
And listens with enchanted mind
As wizard voices in the wind
Sing of his darling native earth,
The rude, the true, the hardy north !

His native dales, his native streams,—
The angels of his exile-dreams,—
Each dingle green, each breezy height,
Awakes his spirit to delight.
Oh, welcome to the fresh old hills !
The mossy crags, the tinkling rills,—
To field, and wood, and moorland glen,
Welcome, welcome home again !

Well may the pleasant summer air
Fondly play with thy silver hair ;
Well may the brooklet's ripples clear
Leap as thy footsteps wander near ;
Well may the wild-flowers on the lea,
Nodding their pretty heads to thee,
Scatter abroad their sweetest sweet,

Their fond old poet friend to meet ;—
They've waited, and have listened long,
For thee, oh, white-haired son of song !

Though tempests rage and clouds are black,
The sun keeps on his glorious track,
Serenely shining, to the west,
And, grandly smiling, sinks to rest.
Thy task, old bard, is nearly done :
Oh, may the evening coming on,
Long lingering sweetly round thy way,
Close like a cloudless summer day !

Poor Travellers All.

I.

POOR travellers all,
Both great and small,
How thoughtlessly we play
In a country
Of mortality,
Where never a man can stay.

II.

Our birth is but
A starting foot
Upon the fatal road,
Where death keeps watch
O'er life, to snatch
The jewel back to God.

III.

Time's sickle reaps,
In restless sweeps,
The harvest of decay;
On every ground
His sheaves are bound,
And garnered in the clay.

IV.

Though hints divine,
In symbols fine,
With warnings strew the way,—
Beseeching us,
And teaching us,
The danger of delay,—

V.

We dally still,
With fitful will,
Among delusive joys;
Heeding them not,
Except for sport,—
As children play with toys.

VI.

We romp and run
Mad in the sun;
We murmur at the cloud;
And where's the breast
That's quite at rest
Until it's in a shroud?

VII.

Poor travellers all,
Both great and small,
How thoughtlessly we play,
In a country
Of mortality,
Where never a man can stay.

What Makes Your Leaves Fall Down?*

I.

WHAT makes your leaves fall down,
Ye drooping autumn flowers?
What makes your green go brown,
Ye fading autumn bowers?
Oh, thou complaining gale,
That wand'rest sad and lone,
What sorrows swell the tale
Of that funereal moan?

II.

Have ye felt love like mine,
And met with like return,
That ye do thus decline,
And thus appear to mourn?
Ah, no! content, methinks,
Ye glide into decay,
As pensive evening sinks
At close of summer day.

III.

Fall down, ye leafy bowers!
And drift upon the gales;
Fade on, ye sleepy flowers!
It is my heart that wails;
Blow on, thou quiet wind!
It was a fancied moan—
The echo of a mind
That feels its pleasure gone.

* Published with music, by Messrs. Hime and Addison, Manchester.

Alas! How Hard it is to Smile.

I.

ALAS! how hard it is to smile
When all within is sad;
And rooted sorrow to beguile
By mingling with the glad.
The heart that swells with grief disdains
Pretension's mean alloy,
And feels far less its keenest pains
Than mockeries of joy.

II.

How few among the thoughtless crowds
Can tell the jealous care
With which a gentle spirit shrouds
Its pangs from worldly glare.
The harp of sorrow wooes the touch
Of sympathy alone;
Its trembling fibres shrink from such
As cannot feel their tone.

III.

The gay may sport upon the wave
Of life's untroubled tides,—
Like birds that warble on a grave,
They dream not what it hides;
But pleasure's wretched masquerade
Wakes sorrow's keenest throe;—
The saddest look is not so sad
As the strainèd smile of woe.

The Man of the Time.

I.

HE is a sterling nobleman
Who lives the truth he knows;
Who dreads the slavery of sin,
And fears no other foes.

II.

Who scorns the folly of pretence;
Whose mind from cant is free;
Who values men for worth and sense,
And hates hypocrisy.

III.

Who glows with love that's free from taint;
Whose heart is kind and brave;
Who feels that he was neither meant
For tyrant nor for slave.

IV.

Who loves the ground, where'er he roam,
That's trod by human feet,
And strives to make the world a home
Where peace and justice meet.

V.

Whose soul to clearer heights can climb,
  Above the shows of things,—
Cleaving the mortal bounds of time,
  On meditative wings.

VI.

Malice can never mar his fame;
  A heaven-crowned king is he;
His robe, a pure immortal aim;
  His throne, eternity.

The Wanderer's Hymn.*

I.

HAPPY the heart that's simply pure;
  Happy the heart that's nobly brave;
Happy the man that breaks the lure
  That winds like death round folly's slave.

II.

Wandering in the worldly throng,
  The dust of earth still keeps us blind;
The judgment's weak, the passion's strong,
  The will as fitful as the wind.

III.

Disguised in joy's deceitful beams,
A thousand fitful meteors ply
About our path the demon-schemes,
That dazzle only to destroy.

IV.

Who can we ask for aid but Thee,
Our only friend, our only guide?
What other counsellor have we?
Where else, oh, where, can we abide?

V.

Oh! hear and help us while we pray;
And travel with us all the way!
Oh! hold our hands, and be our stay!
Oh! set us right whene'er we stray!

* Published with music, by Messrs. Hime and Addison, Manchester.

Alone, upon the Flowery Plain.

I.

ALONE, upon the flowery plain,
I rove, in solitary pain;
Looking around the silent lea
For something I shall never see.

II.

Yon hedge-row blossoms as before,
And roses shade yon cottage door;
But oh, I miss the tresses fair,
And eyes that glowed with welcome there.

III.

The streamlet, still, in rippling pranks,
Kisses the wild flower on its banks;
But I am lonely on the shore,
To which my love returns no more.

IV.

The lark, aloft in sunny air,
Carols, as if my love was there;
And the wind goes by, with mournful sound,
Murmuring, "No more, on mortal ground."

To a Young Lady,

WHO LENT ME AN OLD BOOK.

I.

THIS learnèd volume doth not tell
A story so divine,
Nor point a moral half so well
As that young face of thine.

II.

Thou should'st have sent a rose to me,
With morning dew bestarred ;
It would have better likened thee,—
Sweet rosebud of the bard !

III.

But mornings fly, and dewdrops dry,
And many a lovely rose
Is plucked, and thrown neglected by,
Before it fairly blows.

IV.

Elsie ; thy budding time is fair ;
So may thy blooming be ;
And never blighting blast of care
Untimely wither thee.

V.

Flower on, in gladness, free from stain,
Until the autumn's past ;
And, like a fading rose, retain
Thy sweetness to the last.

Oh! Weave a Garland for my Brow.

I.

OH! weave a garland for my brow,
Of roses and of rue;
For once I loved a bonny lass,—
Alas, she was not true!
But when she slighted all my grief,
I knew that grief was vain,
And I hid the wound that pained my heart,
Until it healed again.

II.

Then, gentle lover, pine no more,—
Thy tenderness is blind;
Sighing to one whose heart is cold
Will never make her kind.
Go, take some comfort to thy breast—
The world is fair to see—
And on some genial bosom rest
Whose pulses beat for thee.

To the Spring Wind.

I.

SWEET minstrel of the scented spring,
Ten thousand silver bells,
To welcome thee, are all a-swing,
Upon the dewy fells
To sing with thee, I should be fain,
Oh, harper blithe and free!
But love has bound me with a chain,
That wrings the heart of me.

II.

Oh, hasten to my love, and tell
Her how she makes me pine;
And ask her if she thinks it well
To slight a heart like mine;
For, if my suit her scorn doth move,
It shall no longer be;
Although I know she's made for love,
And I wish that she loved me.

Oh! Had She Been a Lowly Maid.*

I.

OH! had she been a lowly maid
That stole this heart of mine,
She would have filled the humblest shade
With radiance divine :—
The moon of beauty's starry skies,
She glides serenely fair,
Absorbing in her gleaming eyes
The brightest planet there.

II.

Oh! were she but a flower of spring
Upon the dewy lea,
To watch its lovely blossoming
My heart's delight would be;
And when its leaves began to fade,
Their fading I would moan;
And treasure up the sacred dust,
To mingle with my own.

* Published with music, by Messrs. Hime and Addison, Manchester.

All On a Rosy Morn of June.*

I.

ALL on a rosy morn of June,
When farmers make their hay,
Down by yon bonny woodland green
A milking maid did stray;
And oh, but she was sweet and fair,—
The flower of all the vale;
In her hand a wild white rose she bare,
And on her head a pail.

II.

Across the fields, as she did rove.
The pretty maiden sang
A plaintive lay of tender love
That through the valley rang:
Blithe as a linnet on the spray,
Among the wildwood green,
She lilted on her flowery way,—
And vanished from the scene.

III.

When next I saw that pleasant vale—
Twelve moons had wandered by—
A matron told her hapless tale
With tear-drops in her eye;
For there had been, with winsome wile,
A careless-hearted lad,
And plucked the flower whose lovely smile
Made all the valley glad.

* Published with music, by Messrs. Hime aud Addison, Manchester.

IV.

The woods were gay and green again;
  The sun was smiling on;
But the charmer of the rural glen
  For evermore was gone:
Now, mouldering near the churchyard way,
  All stricken in her pride,
The white rose of the valley lay,
  With an infant by her side.

Glad Welcome to Morn's Dewy Hours.

I.

GLAD welcome to morn's dewy hours
The birds warble blithe to the gale,
While the sun shimmers through the green bowers,
And plays with the stream in the vale;
But, as clouds o'er the heavens come streaming,
Then silence, with shade, creeps along:
They pass,—and again the woods gleaming,
At once wake to sunlight and song.

II.

So I sport till the storm gathers o'er me;
Then pensively hushed in the gloom,
My heart looks around and before me,
For something the shade to illume;
Yet, though folding the wings of my gladness,
I'm mute in the hurricane's howl,
Thou com'st, through the gloomiest sadness,
A sunbeam of joy to my soul.

III.

Fair star of remembrance endearing,
Still lend me thy brilliant ray,
My wanderings chast'ning and cheering,
Till life with its life fade away;
And, oft as my pathway thou greetest,
I'll waken my harp-strings to thee,
And sing how the brightest and sweetest
Are always the soonest to flee.

When Drowsy Daylight.

I.

WHEN drowsy daylight's drooping e'e
Closes o'er the fading lea,—
When evening hums his vesper-song,
And winking dews the meadow throng,
I'll come to meet thee, Mary!

II.

The lazy hours refuse to fly;
As gaudy day goes creeping by,
I count each moment with a sigh,
Until the hour of shade steals nigh,
That brings me to my Mary!

III.

The flower is dear unto the lea,
The blossom to the parent tree:—
Thou'rt more than flower and leaf to me—
This heart of mine, by love of thee,
Must bloom or wither, Mary.

IV.

The summer woods are waving fair;
The bluebell scents the evening air;
The small bird woos its mate to share
Its little nest and loving care:—
Oh, be my own, my Mary!

Ye Gallant Men of England.

I.

YE gallant men of England,
Of noble races bred,
Remember how your fathers
For liberty have bled;
Stand to your ancient banners,
In a thousand battles torn,—
The banners of Great Britain,
To a thousand victories borne.

II.

When flags of tyrants, flying,
Insult the air again,
And freedom's sons are dying
Upon the bloody plain,
Rush to the gory havoc
With all your native might,
And carve your way to justice,
Or perish for the right.

III.

Ye sons of ancient heroes,
And heirs of England's fame,
Wherever danger threatens
Be worthy of your name;
And hurl each bold aggressor
Into his native lair,
To rule the slaves and traitors
That crawl around him there.

IV.

Though knaves and cowards tremble
  Beneath despotic sway,
And fools to wily tyrants
  Resign, a willing prey,
The race of island lions,
  Bred by the Western main,
The freedom won by battle
  By battle can maintain.

Prologue.

(WRITTEN ON THE OCCASION OF THE MANCHESTER LETTERPRESS PRINTERS' DRAMATIC ENTERTAINMENT, APRIL 4TH, 1868.)

WHEN first, from old Westminster's hoary pile,
The Art of Printing dawned on Briton's isle,
In some dim chapel of that sacred fane
The venerable Caxton ruled his train,—
Whose artful toil, foredoomed by mystic tie,
Flushed the young stream of England's liberty.
England! where noble hearts had wrestled long,
In dumb contention between right and wrong,
'Twas there in cloistered shade, he wove the spell
At whose behest the chain of silence fell;
And, nursing skill, with strange mutations fraught,
Gave freedom to the prisoned realms of thought!

. . . . . .

Strange were the implements, the labour strange;
The little rill of art was big with change;
With loving care, the initiated few
There brought the infant mystery to view;
And, as in dim secluded gloom they toiled,
Fate's folded skein of printed thought uncoiled;
Whilst the hushed murmurs of the working throng
Mingled with solemn strains of sacred song:

There learned churchmen pondered in amaze,
And kingly patrons dealt bewildered praise:
Ah, little dreamt they what that germ contained,—
What vast, upheaving powers, heaven-ordained!

. . . . . .

Rude were the artist's tools, the product slight;
Costly and few the works it brought to light;
Mysterious came the first imprinted page,
To th' wondering gaze of an unletter'd age;
And small the inducement such an art to ply,
When only clerks could read, and only kings could buy.

But time,—the soil of life's eventful field,—
Was doomed, by fate, the mighty plant to yield;
Doomed to sustain, and nurture, through the night
Of undergrowth, until it burst to sight,
And cheered the nations with its presence bright!
Slow grew the art,—though often checked,—it *grew*;
Now, nipt with frost, now fed with rain and dew;
Slow grew the struggling art, but *yet* it *grew*.
In patient majesty the nursling rose;
Rooted by struggle, and made strong by blows;

Till e'en its nurses watched it with surprise,
And tyrants trembled as they saw it rise!
For, as it grew, to realms of light it led,
And fed the freedom upon which it fed.
Oh, freedom! Spark of heaven-descended fire,
That never fades from noble heart's desire!
The bird that in the wild wood carols free,—
No bird, imprisoned, sings so well as he!
Thanks to those lofty stars of England's night,
Who cheered her struggling sons with steadfast light!
Thanks to the men who fought and suffered long,
To make the right triumphant over wrong.
Thanks to those gallant hearts of later breed,
By whom the Press was from its trammels freed.—
Now, thousands print what millions rush to read.

But stay, my roving muse,—restrain thy flight,
What is it brings the Press-gang here to-night?
Come they, as erst, some wandering slave to seize?
Ah, no,—*our* mission is to free, and please:
In mutual self-reliance to combine,
To soothe the last sad hours of life's decline;
To help the feeble and to cheer the sad;
The worn-out workman's sinking heart to glad;
From bitter penury the sick to save,
And soothe the totterer's way unto the grave.
And feeble though our histrionic skill,
It humbly seeks to lessen human ill.
Then, oh, with generous hearts, give kind acclaim,
And cheer the labour for its noble aim.

Oh, Printing, Art with mystic power fraught!
Thou swift dispenser of undying thought!
Strew lofty lessons still, at heaven's behest:
And teach us Charity above the rest!
And, till we're summoned hence, by fatal call,—
Father of Nature's Chapel,* bless us all!

---

* In the old printing-offices of England, and even in many of the best printing-offices of the kingdom now, the workmen form a little court of law, summoned occasionally for the settlement of disputes among themselves. This court they call "The Chapel," and the President of the court is called "The Father of the Chapel." Doubtless these names arise from the tradition that the first English printing-office was in one of the chapels of Westminster Abbey.

LANCASHIRE SONGS

Come Whoam to Thy Childer an' Me.*

I.

AW'VE just mended th' fire wi' a cob;[1]
Owd Swaddle has brought thi new shoon;
There's some nice bacon-collops o'th hob,
An' a quart o' ale posset i'th oon;[2]
Aw've brought thi top-cwot,[3] doesto know,
For th' rain's comin' deawn very dree;[4]
An' th' har'stone's as white as new snow;—
Come whoam to thi childer an' me.

* Published with music, by Messrs. Hime and Addison, Manchester.

[1] *Cob*, a lump of coal.
[2] *Oon*, oven.
[3] *Top-cwot*, top-coat.
[4] *Dree*, wearily-continuous.

II.

When aw put little Sally to bed,
  Hoo cried, 'cose her feyther[1] weren't theer,
So aw kiss'd th' little thing, an' aw said
  Thae'd bring her a ribbin fro' th' fair;

An' aw gav her her doll, an' some rags,
  An' a nice little white cotton-bo';
An' aw kiss'd her again; but hoo said
  'At hoo wanted to kiss *thee* an' o'.

III.

An' Dick, too, aw'd sich wark wi' him,
  Afore aw could get him up stairs;
Thae towd him thae'd bring him a drum,
  He said, when he're sayin' his prayers;
Then he looked i' my face, an' he said,
  "Has th' boggarts taen houd o' my dad?"
An' he cried till his een were quite red;—
  He likes thee some weel, does yon lad!

---

[1] *Feyther*, father.

IV.

At th' lung-length, aw geet 'em laid still;
An' aw hearken't folks' feet that went by;
So aw iron't o' my clooas reet well,
An aw hanged 'em o'th maiden to dry;
When aw'd mended thi stockin's an' shirts,
Aw sit deawn to knit i' my cheer,
An' aw rayley did feel rayther hurt,—
Mon, aw'm *one-ly* when theaw artn't theer.

V.

"Aw've a drum an' a trumpet for Dick;
Aw've a yard o' blue ribbin for Sal;
Aw've a book full o' babs;[1] an' a stick
An' some bacco an' pipes for mysel';
Aw've brought thee some coffee an' tay,—
Iv thae'll *feel* i' my pocket, thae'll *see;*
An' aw've bought tho a new cap to-day,—
But aw al'ays bring summat for *thee!*

VI.

"God bless tho', my lass; aw'll go whoam,[2]
An' aw'll kiss thee an' th' childer o' round;
Thae knows, that wherever aw roam,
Aw'm fain to get back to th' owd ground;
Aw can do wi' a crack o'er a glass;
Aw can do wi' a bit of a spree;
But aw've no gradely[3] comfort, my lass,
Except wi' yon childer and thee."

---

[1] *Babs*, babies, pictures.
[2] *Whoam*, home.
[3] *Gradely*, proper, right.

What Ails Thee, My Son Robin?*

I.

WHAT ails thee, my son Robin?
My heart is sore for thee;
Thi cheeks are grooin' thinner,
An' th' leet has laft thi e'e;[1]
Theaw trails abeawt so lonesome,
An' looks so pale at morn;
God bless tho, lad, aw'm soory[2]
To see tho so forlorn.

II.

Thi fuustep's sadly awter't,[3]—
Aw used to know it weel,—
Neaw, arto fairy-stricken, lad;
Or, arto gradely[4] ill?
Or, hasto bin wi' th' witches
I'th cloof,[5] at deep o'th neet?
Come, tell mo, Robin, tell mo,—
For summat is not reet!

III.

"Eh, mother, dunnut fret yo;
Aw am not like mysel';
But, 'tisn't lung o'th feeorin'[1]
That han to do wi' th' deil;
There's nought 'at thus could daunt mo,
I'th cloof, by neet nor day;—
It's yon blue een o' Mary's;—
They taen my life away."

---

* Published with music, by Messrs. Hime and Addison, Manchester.

[1] *Th' leet has laft thi e'e,* the light has left thine eye.

[2] *Soory,* sorry.

[3] *Awter't,* altered.

[4] *Gradely,* properly, thoroughly.

[5] *Cloof,* clough, glen.

IV.

"Aw deawt[2] aw've done wi comfort
 To th' day that aw mun dee,
For th' place hoo sets her fuut on,
 It's fairy greawnd[3] to me;
But, oh, it's no use speykin',
 Aw connut ston her pride;
An' when a true heart's breykin'
 It's very hard to bide!"

V.

Neaw, God be wi' tho, Robin;
 Just let her have her way;
Hoo'll never meet thy marrow,[4]
 For mony a summer day;
Aw're just same wi' thi feyther,
 When first he spoke to me:
So, go thi ways, an' whistle;
 An' th' lass'll come to thee!

[1] *Feeorin'*, frightening, things that frighten.
[2] *Aw deawt*, I doubt, I think, I surmise.
[3] *Fairy-greawnd*, enchanted ground.
[4] *Marrow*, match.

The Grindlestone.

I.

IT wur Dody o' Joseph's, a joiner by trade,
A comical cowt, and a keen-bitten blade,
He're as fause as a boggart, as th' neighbours
weel knew,
Though, when he'd a mind, he could look like a foo'.
Derry down.

II.

But th' bravest and breetest o'th childer o' men,
May haply be hamper't a bit now an' then ;
Dody's axe wanted grindin', one wark-a-day morn,
When there nob'dy about to gi' th' grindle a turn.
Derry down.

III.

Then he grunted, an' mumble't, an' glendur't around,
An' he tooted about o'er the neighbourin' ground;
Still, never a soul to turn th' stone could he find,
An' it made him a little bit thrutched in his mind.
Derry down.

IV.

Till a soft-lookin' urchin coom wanderin' by,
Wi' his thumb in his mouth, an' a tear in his eye;
Wi' his slate an' his satchel, he're creepin' to schoo',
An',—bi th' look of his een,—Dody know'd he're a foo'.
Derry down.

V.

"Bi th' maskins," says Dody, "I'm losen't at last!"
An' he beckon't o'th lad that wur wanderin' past!
"Come hither, my tight little maister o' men!"
Then he poo'd out a sixpence,—an' fobbed it again.
Derry down.

VI.

"There's a grindlestone here—dosto think thou can turn;
If thou does'nt know how, I can help tho to larn.
I connot howd th' axe an' turn th' hondle mysel';
Thou'rt a nice lad o' somebry's—come, give us a twell!"
Derry down.

VI.

Th' lad laid howd o'th hondle, an' shap't like a mon;
For he lippen't o' sixpence, when th' turning wur done;
So, he twirl't at this grindle o' Dody o' Joe's,
Till saut-water trickl't off th' end of his nose.
Derry down.

VIII.

Dody felt at his axe,—an' he said, "Thou young foo';
Thou'lt get a rare twiltin' for stoppin' fro' schoo';
Hie tho' off, like a red-shank, or th' dur may be teen'd:"
An' he gav' him a bit of a lifter beheend.
Derry down.

IX.

Th' lad dried fro his for-yed the breet briny drip;
An' he pike'd up his books, wi' a wimperin' lip;
An' he crope off to schoo', turnin' o'er in his mind
Th' first lesson he'd larn't i' the pranks o' monkind.
Derry down.

X.

As yo wander'n through life, ten 'at one that yo'n find
A good lot o' folk that han axes to grind;
Give a turn when yo con; but remember to th' end,
It's turnin' th' wrang road to turn on a friend.
Derry down.

God Bless these Poor Folk.*

I.

GOD bless these poor folk that are strivin'
By means that are honest an' true,
For some'at[1] to keep 'em alive in
This world that we're scramblin' through:
As th' life ov a mon's full o' feightin',[2]
A poor soul that wants to feight fair,
Should never be grudged ov his heytin',[3]
For th' hardest o'th battle's his share.
CHORUS—As th' life ov a mon.

II.

This world's kin to trouble; i'th best on't,
There's mony sad changes come reawnd;
We wandern abeawt to find rest on't,
An' th' worm yammers[4] for us i'th greawnd.
May he that'll wortch[1] while he's able,
Be never long hungry nor dry;
An' th' childer 'at sit at his table,—
God bless 'em wi' plenty, say I.
CHORUS—As th' life ov a mon.

III.

An' he that can feel it a pleasur'
To leeten misfortin an' pain,—
May his pantry be olez full measur',
To cut at, and come to again;
May God bless his cup and his cupbort,[2]

---

* Published with music, by Messrs. Hime and Addison, Manchester.

[1] *Some'at*, somewhat. [2] *Feightin'*, fighting. [3] *Heytin*, eating.
[4] *Yammer*, to make an eager noise with the jaws, like hungry children at meal-time.

A theawsan' for one that he gives;
An' his heart be a bumper o' comfort,
To th' very last minute he lives!
CHORUS—As th' life ov a mon.

IV.

An' he that scorns ale to his victual,
Is welcome to let it alone;
There's some can be wise with a little,
An' some that are foolish wi' noan;
An' some are so quare i' their natur,
That nought wi' their stomachs agree;
But, he that would leifer[3] drink wayter,
Shall never be stinted by me.
CHORUS—As th' life ov a mon.

V.

One likes to see hearty folk wortchin',
An' weary folk havin' a rest;
One likes to yer poor women singin'
To th' little things laid o' their breast:
Good cooks are my favourite doctors;
Good livers my parsons shall be;
An' ony poor craytur at's clemmin,[1]
May come have a meawthful wi' me.
CHORUS.—As th' life ov a mon.

VI.

Owd Time,—he's a troublesome codger,—
Keeps nudgin'[2] us on to decay,
An' whispers, "Yo're nobbut[3] a lodger;
Get ready for goin' away;"
Then let's ha' no skulkin' nor sniv'lin',
Whatever misfortins befo';
God bless him that fends[4] for his livin',
An' houds up his yed[5] through it o'!
CHORUS.—As th' life ov a mon.

Come, Mary, Link Thi Arm i' Mine.*

I.

COME, Mary, link thi arm i' mine,
An' lilt away wi' me;
An' dry that little drop o' brine,
Fro' th' corner o' thi e'e;
Th' mornin' dew i'th heather-bell's
A bonny bit o' weet;
That tear a different story tells,—
It pains my heart to see't.
So, Mary, link thi arm i' mine.

II.

No lordly ho' o'th country side's
So pleasant to my view,
As th' little corner where abides
My bonny lass an' true;
But there's a nook beside yon spring,—
An' if theaw'll share't wi' me;
Aw'll buy tho th' bonny'st gowden ring
That ever theaw did see!
So, Mary, link thi arm i' mine.

III.

My feyther's gan mo forty peawnd,
I' silver an' i' gowd;
An' a pratty bit o' garden greawnd,
O' th' mornin' side o'th fowd;
An' a honsome bible, clen an' new,
To read for days to come;—
There's leaves for writin' names in, too,
Like th' owd un at's awhoam.
So, Mary, link thi arm i' mine.

IV.

Eawr Jenny's bin a-buyin' in,
  An' every day hoo brings
Knives an' forks, an' pots ; an' irons
  For smoothin' caps an' things ;
My gronny's sent a kist o' drawers,
  Sunday clooas to keep ;
An' little Fanny's bought a glass
  Where thee an' me can peep.
      So, Mary, link thi arm i' mine.

V.

Eawr Tum has sent a bacon-flitch ;
  Eawr Jem a load o' coals ;
Eawr Charlie's bought some pickters, an'
  He's hanged 'em upo' th' woles ;
Owd Posy's white-weshed th' cottage through ;
  Eawr Matty's made it sweet ;
An Jack's gan me his Jarman flute,
  To play bi th' fire at neet !
      So, Mary, link thi arm i' mine.

VI.

There's cups an' saucers ; porritch-pons,
  An' tables, greyt an' smo' ;
There's brushes, mugs, an' ladin'-cans ;
  An eight-day's clock an' o' ;
There's a cheer[2] for thee, an' one for me,
  An' one i' every nook ;
Thi mother's has a cushion on't,—
  It 's th' nicest cheer i'th rook.[3]
      So, Mary, link thi arm i' mine.

VII.

My gronny's gan me th' four-post bed,
  Wi' curtains to 't an' o' ;
An' pillows, sheets, an' bowsters, too,

As white as driven snow;
It isn't stuffed wi' fither-deawn,
But th' flocks are clen an' new;
Hoo says there 's honest folk i'th teawn
That 's made a warse un[5] do.
So, Mary, link thi arm i' mine.

VIII.

Aw peeped into my cot last neet;
It made me hutchin' fain;
A bonny fire were winkin' breet
I' every window-pane;
Aw marlocked upo' th' white hearth-stone,
An' drummed o'th kettle lid;
An' sung, "My neest[4] is snug an' sweet;
Aw'll go and fotch my brid[5]!"
So, Mary, link thi arm i' mine.

Chirrup.

I

YOUNG Chirrup wur a mettled cowt :[1]
His heart an' limbs wur true ;
At foot race, or at wrostlin'-beawt,
Or aught he buckled to ;
At wark or play, reet gallantly
He laid into his game :
An' he're very fond o' singin'-brids,[2]—
That's heaw he geet his name.

II.

He're straight as ony pickin'-rod,[1]
An' limber as a snig :[2]
An' th' heartiest cock o'th village clod,
At ony country rig :
His shinin' een wur clear an' blue ;
His face wur frank an' bowd ;
An' th' yure abeawt his monly broo[3]
Wur crispt i' curls o' gowd.

III.

Young Chirrup donned his clinker't shoon,[4]
An' startin' off to th' fair,
He swore by th' leet o'th harvest moon,
He'd have a marlock[5] there;
He poo'd a sprig fro th' hawthorn-tree,
That blossomed by the way;—
"Iv ony mon says wrang[6] to me,
Aw 'll tan his hide to-day!"

IV.

Full sadly mony a lass would sigh,
As wand'rin' slyly near,
They tooted at his een to spy
Iv love wur lurkin' theer;
So fair an' free he stept the green,
An' trollin' eawt a song,
Wi' leetsome heart, an' twinklin' een,
Went chirrupin' along.

V.

Young Chirrup woo'd a village maid,—
An' hoo wur th' flower ov o',—
Wi' kisses kind, i'th woodlan' shade,
An' whispers soft an' low;
I' Mally's ear twur th' sweetest chime
That ever mortal sung;
An' Mally's heart beat merry time
To th' music ov his tung.

VI.

The kindest mates, this world within,
Mun sometimes meet wi' pain;
But, iv this pain could life begin,
They'd buckle to again;
For, though he're hearty, blunt, an' tough,
An' Mally sweet an' mild,
For three-score year, through smooth an' rough,
Hoo lad him like a child.

The Dule's i' this Bonnet o' Mine.*

I.

THE dule's i' this bonnet o' mine;
My ribbins 'll never be reet;
Here, Mally, aw'm like to be fine,
For Jamie 'll be comin' to-neet;
He met me i'th lone[1] tother day,—
Aw're gooin' for wayter[2] to th' well,—
An' he begged that aw'd wed him i' May;—
Bi' th mass,[3] iv he'll let me, aw will.

II.

When he took my two honds into his,
Good Lord, heaw they trembled between;
An' aw durstn't look up in his face,
Becose[4] on him seein' my e'en;
My cheek went as red as a rose;—
There's never a mortal can tell
Heaw happy aw felt; for, thea knows,
Aw couldn't ha' axed[5] him mysel'.

III.

But th' tale wur at th' end o' my tung,—
To let it eawt wouldn't be reet,—
For aw thought to seem forrud[1] wur wrong,
So aw towd him aw'd tell him to-neet;
But, Mally, thae knows very weel,—
Though it isn't a thing one should own,—
If aw'd th' pikein'[2] o'th world to mysel',
Aw'd oather[3] ha' Jamie or noan.

---

* Published with music, by Messrs. Hine and Addison, Manchester.

[1] *Lone*, lane. [2] *Wayter*, water.

[3] *Bi'th mass*, by the mass; an expression brought down from Catholic times.

[4] *Becose*, because. [5] *Axed*, asked.

IV.

Neaw, Mally, aw've towd tho my mind ;
What wouldto do iv 'twur thee ?
" Aw'd tak him just while he're inclined,
An' a farrantly bargain[4] he'd be ;
For Jamie's as gradely[5] a lad
As ever stept eawt into th' sun ;—
So, jump at thy chance, an' get wed,
An' do th' best tho con, when it's done ! "

V.

Eh, dear, but it's time to be gwon,—
Aw should'nt like Jamie to wait,—
Aw connut for shame be too soon,
An' aw wouldn't for th' world be to late ;
Aw'm o' ov a tremble too th' heel,—
Dost think at my bonnet 'll do ?
" Be off, lass,—thae looks very weel ;—
He wants noan o'th bonnet, thae foo ! "

---

[1] *Forrud*, forward. [2] *Pikein'*, picking, choosing. [3] *Oather*, either.
[4] *A farrantly bargain*, a decent bargain, a good bargain.
[5] *Gradely*, proper, right.

Willy-Ground.

AIR—" *The Night before Larry was Stretched.*"

I.

COME, Caleb, an' sattle thi shanks,
An' let's ha' no moore o' thi bother ;
Wi' thi camplin' din, an' thi pranks,
Thou'rt wortchin' thisel' to a lother.
Come, Nathan, poo up into th' nook,—
I know thou'rt a comical crayter ;
Let's join at a conk, an' a smooke,
An' a bumper o' whot rum an' wayter.
Fal-lal-der-dal.

II.

We're neighbours, an' very weel met ;
We're o' merry lads, o' good mettle ;
Here's Nathan,—wur never licked yet,—
An' Caleb's i' farrantly fettle.
Wi' a pipe, an' a tot, an' a crack,
An' a crony, I'm just i' my glory ;
So now, I'll tip th' world fro' my back,
An' brast off wi' a bit of a story.
Fal-lal-der-dal.

III.

Tother day, as I're rovin' areawt,
I let of owd Robin o' Bumper's ;
He's a terrible gullet for grout,—
An', at poachin', they say'n he's a crumper ;
But, he's good at a tot an' a tale ;
So, we popt into Peter o' Nancy's,

An' I said to him, " Co' for some ale,
  Or aught i' this hole 'at thou fancies."
    Fal-lal-der-dal.

IV.

As we crope wi' er gills up to th' hob,
  Th' owd layrock began for to twitter ;
An' he towd of a ticklesome job,
  At' sent us o' into a titter ;
One day, when he're prickin' a hare
  A bit of a wacker coom o'er him,
For, just as he're settin' a snare,
  Th' owd owner o'th lond stoode afore him.
    Fal-lal-der-dal.

V.

" Hollo ; what are you doing here ? "
  Says Robin, "Why, nought nobbut walkin' ;"
" Walk off, then ! " cried he, with a sneer ;
  "This land belongs me, where you're stalking !"
Says Robin, " Yo're reet, I'll be bound ;
  But, what's to be done, I can't tell, sir ;
For, I'm like to walk somebody's ground,
  As I've noan 'at belungs to mysel', sir."
    Fal-lal-der-dal.

VI.

This lond,—it's a ticklesome lot ;
  To wrangle about it's a blunder ;
For, whether one owns it or not,
  He'll very soon ha' to knock under ;
Both lonlords an' tenants mun flit ;
  Let's hope, without fratchin', or frownin',
They'n let us walk on it a bit,
  An' then lend us a bit to lie down in.
    Fal-lal-der-dal, layrol-i-day.

A Bit of a Sing.

I.

BILL o' Sheepsheawter's;
Robin o'th Dree;
Rondle o' Scouter's;
Twilter, an' me;
We made Mally Grime's
Owd kitchen roof ring,
One merry yule-time,
When met for to sing!
Tooral-loo; falder-day!

II.

Rondle sang counter;
Robin sang bass;
Twilter sang o' maks
O' comical ways;
Th' tenor wur fine,—
Bill took it up well;
An' th' treble wur mine,—
I sang it mysel'!
Tooral-loo; falder-day!

III.

Th' first wur a psalm;
An' th' next wur a sung;
An' then we sang glees,
Till th' rack-an'-hook rung;
An' merry owd Mall
Chime't in, like a brid,
As hoo tinkle't to th' tune,
Upo' th' owd kettle lid.
Tooral-loo; falder-day!

IV.

"Stop, an' rosin!" cried Bill,
"It's gettin' hee time!"
"Weet yor whistles!" said Mall,
"It sweetens the chime!"
"A tot a-piece bring!"
Cried Rondle, "an' then,
Like layrocks o'th wing,
We'n tootle again!"
Tooral-loo; falder-day!

V.

We twitter't an' sang
Till midneet wur gone;
We caper't off whoam,
Bi th' leet o' the moon;
As we wander't o'er th' moss,
Bil lap shoolder-hee;
An', "I'm fain that I'm wick!"
Cried Robin o'th Dree.
Tooral-loo; falder-day!

Tommy Pobs.

AIR—"*Derry Down.*"

I.

TOMMY POBS wur a good-natur't sort of a lad;
He're a weighver by trade, an' he wove for his dad;
He're fond o' down-craiters; an' th' neighbours o' said
That he're reet in his heart, but he'd nought in his yed.
Derry down.

II.

Nan o' Flup's wur a lass that wur swipper an strung;
Hoo'd a temper o' fire, an' a rattlin' tung;
Hoo're as hondsome a filly as mortal e'er see'd,
But hoo coom of a racklesome, natterin' breed.
Derry down.

III.

Nan had fritter't away o' th' for-end of her life,
For hoo'd flirted o' round, though hoo'd ne'er bin a wife;
But, one day, when hoo fund hoo're turn't thirty year owd,
Hoo began a-bein flayed hoo'd be left out i'th cowd.
Derry down.

IV.

Then hoo tooted around among th' lads about whoam,
An' hoo thought hoo'd a bit of a chance wi' poor Tom;
An' hoo cutter't, an' foodle't, an simper't, an skenn'd,
Till hoo geet him as fast as a thief, i' th' far end.
Derry down.

V.

Poor Tom wur so maddle't i' heart and i' yed,
That I doubt he'd ha' dee'd if they hadn't bin wed;
But, at last, they stroke honds, an' agreed to be one;
Nanny tice't him to church—an' poor Tommy wur done.
Derry down.

VI.

An' when th' news o' this weddin' geet down into th' fowd,
Folk chuckle't an' thought that poor Tommy wur sowd;
An' th' women o' said, "Nan's to mich for yon lad;
He'd better ha' stopped till he deẹ'd wi' his dad."
Derry down.

VII.

But they buckle't together, for better an' wur;
An', at first, o' wur reet between Tommy an' hur;
For, they'rn meeterly thick, both bi dayleet an' dark,
Till th' wayter o' life cool't 'em down to their wark.
Derry down.

VIII.

Then, Nanny soon change't, an' coom back to hersel';
An' hoo cample't, an' snapt, as no mortal can tell;
An' poor Tommy Pobs soon fund out that his wife,
Though an angel at first, wur a divole for life.
Derry down.

IX.

Though Nan prove't a blister, an kept him i' pain,
Tom wur like an owd sheep, for he didn't complain:
An' he crope to his looms, an' kept weighvin' away;
But, it made little odds, hoo went warse ev'ry day.
Derry down.

X.

An' hoo hector't, an' plague't him, to sich a degree
That, mony a time, Tom'd ha' bin fain for to dee;
Th' lad did o' that he could to keep thick wi' his wife,
But, it wurn't in her natur' to live a quiet life.
Derry down.

XI.

An', it nettle't her so, that, at last, hoo began
To fling aught at his yed that coom first to her han';
It wur sometimes a pitcher, an' sometimes a pon;
Nanny didn't care what,—if it let o'th owd mon.
Derry down.

XII.

An' if that didn't vex him,—her temper wur sich,—
That hoo'd nip up a tough-lookin' lump of a switch;
An' sometimes it lapt round his hide wi' a bend,
An' sometimes it coom across Tommy's nose-end.
Derry down.

XIII.

An' thus, year by year, this poor couple toar't on,
Till Tommy had groon a grey-yedded owd mon;
Then, Nanny took ill, an' wur laid up i' bed,
An' hoo flang no moore pots at owd Tommy's white yed.
Derry down.

XIV.

At last, Nanny dee'd; an' th' owd lad felt it sore;
For, if hoo'd bin an angel, he'd not ha' grieve't more;
So, he linger't by th' grave till they'd happed her up well;
An' then he coom cryin' away by his-sel.
Derry down.

Toddlin' Whoam.

I.

TODDLIN' whoam fro th' market rant;
Toddlin' whoam, content an' cant;
Wi' mi yed i' my hat, an' my feet i' my shoon;
I'm fain to be toddlin' whoam.

II.

Toddlin' whoam, for th' fireside bliss,
Toddlin' whoam, for th' childer's kiss;
God bless yon bit o' curlin' smooke;
God bless yon cosy chimbley nook!
I'm fain to be toddlin' whoam.

III.

Toddlin' whoam for twitterin' sungs;
Toddlin' whoam for prattlin' tungs;
Toddlin' whoam, to sink to rest
Wi' th' wife, an' little brids i'th nest.
I'm fain to be toddlin' whoam.

Th' Sweetheart Gate.

I.

THERE'S mony a gate[1] eawt of eawr teawn-
end,—
But nobbut one[2] for me;
It winds by a rindlin' wayter side,
An' o'er a posied lea;
It wanders into a shady dell;
An' when I've done for th' day,
I never can sattle[3] this heart o' mine,
Beawt[4] walkin' deawn that way.

II.

It's noather[5] garden, nor posied lea,
Nor wayter rindlin'[6] clear;
But deawn i'th vale there's a rosy nook,
An' my true love lives theer:
It's olez[1] summer where th' heart's content,
Tho' wintry winds may blow;
An' there's never a gate[2] so kind to th' fuut,[3]
As th' gate one likes to go.

---

[1] *Gate*, road, way.
[2] *Nobbut one*, nought but one, only one.
[3] *Sattle*, settle, put to rest.
[4] *Beawt*, without.
[5] *Noather*, neither.
[6] *Wayter rindlin'*, water wandering musically.

III.

When I set off o' sweetheartin', I've
  A theawsan' things to say;
But th' very first glent[4] o' yon chimbley-top,
  It drives 'em o' away;
An' when I meet wi' my bonny lass,
  It sets my heart a-jee;—
There's summut i'th leet[5] o' yon two blue e'en
  That plays the dule wi' me!

IV.

When th' layrock's finished his wark aboon,[6]
  An' laid his music by,
He flutters deawn to his mate, an stops
  Till dayleet stirs i'th sky.[7]
Though Matty sends me away at dark,
  I know that hoo's reet[8] full well;—
An' it's how I love a true-hearted lass,
  No mortal tung[9] can tell.

V.

I wish that Michaelmas Day were past,
  When wakin' time comes on;
An' I wish that Candlemas Day were here,
  An' Matty an' me were one:
I wish this wanderin' wark were o'er,—
  This maunderin' to an' fro;
That I could go whoam to my own true love,
  An' stop at neet an' o'.

---

[1] *Olez*, always.
[2] *Gate*, road, path, way.
[3] *To th' fuut*, to the foot.
[4] *Glent*, a glimpse.
[5] *Th' leet*, the light.
[6] *When th' layrock's finished his wark aboon*, when the lark has finished his work above.
[7] *Till dayleet stirs i'th sky*, till the dawning of the day.
[8] *Hoo's reet*, she's right.
[9] *Tung*, tongue.

Owd Enoch.

I.

OWD ENOCH o' Dan's laid his pipe deawn o'th hob,[1]
And his thin fingers played i'th white thatch of his nob;[2]
"I'm gettin' done up," to their Betty he said;
"Dost think thae could doff me,[3] an dad me[4] to bed?"
Derry down, &c.

II.

Then hoo geet him to bed, an' hoo happed him up weel,[1]
An' hoo said to him, "Enoch, lad; heaw doesto feel?"[2]
"These limbs o' mine, Betty,—they're cranky an' sore;[3]
It's time to shut up when one's getten four-score."
Derry down.

---

[1] *Hob*, a ledge, close to the fire-grate.

[2] *White thatch on his nob*, the white hair of his head.

[3] *Doff me*, do off for me, or take off my clothes for me.

[4] *Dad me*, help me by the hand, as a "dad," or father does a little child in its first efforts to walk.

III.

As hoo potter't abeawt[4] his poor winterly pate,
Th' owd crayter 'ooked dreawsily up at his mate,—
"There's nought on me laft, lass,—do o' at tho con,—[5]
But th' cratchinly[6] frame o' what once wur a mon."
Derry down.

IV.

Then he turn't his-sel' o'er, like a chylt tir't wi' play,[7]
An' Betty crept round, while he're dozing away;
As his e'e-lids sank deawn, th' owd lad mutter't "Well done!
I think there's a bit o' sound sleep coming on."
Derry down.

V.

Then hoo thought hoo'd sit by till he'd had his nap o'er,—
If hoo'd sit theer till then, hoo'd ha' risen no more;
For he cool't eawt o'th world, an' his e'en lost their leet,[1]
Like a cinder i'th fire-grate, i'th deeod time o'th neet.[2]
Derry down.

VI.

As Betty sit rockin' bith' side of his bed,
Hoo looked neaw an' then at owd Enoch's white yed;
An' hoo thought to her-sel' that hoo'd not lung to stay
Iv ever th' owd prop of her life should give way.
Derry Down.

VII.

Then, wond'rin' to see him so seawnd an' so still,
Hoo touched Enoch's hond,—an' hoo fund it wur chill;
Says Betty, "He's cowd; I'll put summat moor on!"[3]
But o' wur no use,[4] for Owd Enoch wur gone!
Derry down.

VIII.

An' when they put Enoch to bed deawn i'th greawnd,[1]
A rook o' poor neighbours stoode bare-yedded reawnd;[2]
They dropt sprigs o' rosemary; an' this wur their text:—
"Th' owd crayter's laid by,[3]—we may haply be th' next!"
Derry down.

IX.

So, Betty wur left to toar on bi hersel';[4]
An' heaw hoo poo'd through it no mortal can tell;
But th' doctor dropt in to look at her one day,
When hoo're rockin' bith' side of an odd cup o' tay.[5]
Derry down.

X.

"Well, Betty," said th' doctor, "heaw dun yo get on?
I'm soory to yer 'at yo'n lost yo'r owd mon:
What complaint had he, Betty?" Says hoo, "I caun't tell;
We ne'er had no doctor; he dee'd of his-sel'."[1]
Derry Down.

---

[1] *Deawn i' th' greawnd*, down in the ground.

[2] *Stoode bare-yedded reawnd*, stood bare-headed around.

[3] *Th' owd crayter's laid by*, the old creature is laid aside. The words "owd crayter," are commonly nsed as a phrase of affection.

[4] *To toar on bi her-sel'*, to drag on wearily by herself, or, alone.

[5] *Bith' side of an odd cup o' tay*, by the side of a lonely cup of tea.

XI.

"Ay, Betty," said th' doctor; "there's one thing quite sure;
Owd age is a thing that no physic can cure:
Fate will have her way, lass,—do o' that we con,—
When th' time's up, we's ha' to sign o'er, an' be gone."
Derry down.

XII.

"Both winter an' summer th' owd mower's at wark,
Sidin' folk eawt o' seet, both bi dayleet an' dark?
He's slavin' away while we're snorin' i' bed;
An' he'd slash at a king, if it coom in his yed."
Derry Down.

XIII.

"These sodiurs, an' parsons, an' maisters o' lond,[1]
He lays 'em i'th greawnd, wi' their meawths full o' sond,
Rags or riches, an' owd greasy cap, or a creawn,—
He sarves o' alike,—for he switches 'em deawn."
Derry down.

XIV.

"The mon that's larn't up, an' the mon that's a foo—[2]
It mays little odds, for they both han to goo;[3]
When they come'n within th' swing of his scythe they mun fo',—
If yo'n root amung th' swathe, yo'n find doctors an' o."[4]
Derry Down.

---

[1] *Maisters o' lond*, masters of land, landowners.

[2] *The mon that's larn't-up, an' the mon that's a foo*, the man that i learned-up to the height of possibility, or, that knows everything,—and the man that is a fool.

[3] *It mays little odds, for they both han to goo*, it makes little difference, for they both have to go.

[4] *If yo'n root amung th' swathe, yo'n find doctors an' o'*, if you will examine the swathe left by the scythe of death, you will find that even those whose business it is to save the lives of others, die, like the rest.

Eawr Folk.*

I.

ER Johnny gi's his mind to books ;
Er Abram studies plants,—
He caps the dule[1] for moss an ferns,
An grooin' polyants ;[2]
For aught abeawt mechanickin',
Er Ned's the very lad ;
My uncle Jamie roots i'th stars,[3]
Enough to drive him mad.

II.

Er Alick keeps a badger's shop,[4]
An teyches Sunday schoo' ;[5]
Er Joseph's welly blynt,[6] poor lad :
Er Timothy's—a foo ;

He's tried three different maks[1] o' trades,
An' olez missed his tip ;[2]
But, then, he's th' prattist[3] whistler
That ever cock'd a lip !

---

* Published with music, by Messrs. Hime and Addison, Manchester.

1 *Caps the dule*, beats the devil, or excels the devil.
2 *Grooin' polyants*, cultivating the polyanthus.
3 *Roots i'th stars*, studies astronomy.
4 *A badger's shop*, a grocer's shop.
5 *Teyches Sunday schoo'*, teaches in a Sunday school.
6 *Welly blynt*, well-nigh blind.

1 *Maks*, makes, shapes, kinds.
2 *Missed his tip*, missed his aim, broken down.
3 *Prattist*, prettiest, most pleasing.

III.

Er Matty helps my mother, an'
Hoo sews, an' tents er Joe;
At doin' sums, an' sich as that,
My feyther licks 'em 'o;
Er Charley,—well,—there connot be
Another pate like his,—
It's o' crom-full o' ancientry,
An' Roman haw-pennies!

IV.

Er Tummy's taen to preitchin',—
He's a topper at it, too;
But then,—what's th' use,—er Bill comes in,
An' swears it winnot do;
When t'one's bin strivin' o' he con
To awter wicked men,
Then t'other mays some marlocks,[2] an'
Convarts 'em o'er again.

V.

Er Abel's th' yung'st; an'—next to Joe,—
My mother likes him t' best:
Hoo gi's him brass, aboon his share,
To keep him nicely drest;—
He's gettin' in wi' th' quality,—
An' when his clarkin's done,
He's olez oather[5] cricketin',
Or shootin' wi' a gun.

VI.

My Uncle Sam's a fiddler; an'
I fain could yer him play
Fro' set o' sun till winter neet
Had melted into day;

For eh,—sich glee—sich tenderness—
  Through every changin' part,
It's th' heart that stirs his fiddle,—
  An' his fiddle stirs his heart!

VII.

An', when he touches th' tremblin'-streng,[1]
  It knows his thowt[2] so weel,
It seawnds as if an angel tried
  To tell what angels feel;
An', sometimes, th' wayter in his e'en[3]
  That fun has made to flow,
Can hardly roll away, afore
  It's blent wi' drops o' woe.

VIII.

Then, here's to Jone, an' Ab, an' Ned,
  An' Matty,—an' er Joe,—
An', my feyther, an' my mother; an'
  Er t'other lads an' o';
An' thee, too, owd musicianer,—
  Aw wish lung life to thee,—
A mon that plays a fiddle weel
  Should never awse[4] to dee!

---

[1] *Th' tremblin' streng*, the vibrating fiddle-string.

[2] *Thowt*, thought.

[3] *Th' wayter in his een*, the water in his eyes.

[4] *Should never awse*, should never attempt.

Forgive One Another.

I.

COME here, my bold cronies, I'll not keep yo' lung,—
Come hither, an' hearken to me;
I'll chant yo a neighbourly snatch of a sung,—
An' th' end o' my ditty shall be,—
Let's forgive one another!

II.

We're a wanderin' band, in a ticklesome land,
Where never a mortal can stay,
When yo seen folk 'at's weary, lads, lend 'em a hand,—
An', oh,—as we're joggin' away,—
Let's forgive one another!

III.

This will-o'-the-wisp in a poor body's breast,
It flutters the life of a mon;
It plays him wild marlocks that rob him o' rest,—
A mortal may do what he con,—
Let's forgive one another!

IV.

Like harp-strings, were made of a different tone,
And the minstrel, he sits up aboon;
To him every note of the gamut's weel known,—
Let's hope that he'll keep us i' tune,
To forgive one another!

V.

At neet, when a mother's her childer undrest,
They paddle'n up close to her knee,
To whisper a prayer afore gooin' to rest;
An', th' sweetest o' th' strain, unto me,
Is,—forgive one another!

VI.

Some liken to wrangle o'er nought but a name,
An' who wur their mams an' their dads;
But, gentle or simple, it ends up the same,—
" We're o' Johnny Butter'oth lads!"[1]
Let's forgive one another!

VII.

When thinkin' o' life an' its troublesome way,
We'n very leet need[2] to be proud;
Strike honds while yo're wick; for yo'n not long to stay;
It's late, when yo're lapped in a shreawd,
To forgive one another!

VIII.

An' neaw,—as we never may o' meet again,—
For th' futur' no mortal can see,—
I'll stick to my text, lads; an', as it began,
So th' end o' my ditty shall be,—
Let's forgive one another!

---

1 "*We're 'o Johnny Butter'oth lads*"—a common saying in Lancashire, meaning that we are all God Almighty's children.

2 *Very leet need*, very light need, very little need.

Buckle to.

I.

GOOD lorjus days,[1] what change there is
Upon this mortal ground ;
As time goes flyin' o'er one's yed,[2]
Heaw quarely things come reawnd ;
What ups an' deawns, an' ins an' eawts ;—
What blendin' ill an' well
There is i' one poor crayter's[3] life,—
It is not for to tell !

II.

When mornin' blinks, mon lies an' thinks
Abeawt the comin' day ;
He lays his bits o' schames so sure,
They connot roll astray ;
He cracks his thumbs, an' thinks o'll leet,[1]
Just heaw it's planned to go ;
But when he looks things up at neet,[2]
He seldom finds it so.

---

[1] *Good lorjus days*, Good lord of our days.
[2] *Yed*, head [3] *Crayter*, creature.

---

[1] *Thinks o'll leet*, thinks everything will light or befall.
[2] *Neet*, night.

III.

An' when a storm comes, dark an' leawd,—
  Wi' mony a weary sigh,
He toots abeawt, i'th slifter't cleawd,
  To find a bit o' sky;
He mopes an' moans, he grunts an' groans,
  An' thinks his comfort's o'er;
But, th' minute th' welkin's breet again,
  He's peearter than before.

IV.

Good luck to th' mortal that can ston
  Good luck, beawt bein' preawd;
That keeps his yed fro grooin' whot,—
  His heart fro grooin' cowd;
That walks his chalks, an' heeds no talks,
  But does the best he con;
An' when things are not to his mind,
  Can bide it like a mon.

V.

Then, let's be lowly when it's fine,
  An' cheerful when it's dark;
Mon ne'er wur made to mope an' whine,
  But buckle to his wark;
It sweetens th' air, it leetens care,—
  I never knew it fail:
Go at it, then,—an' let's toe fair;
  Owd Time 'll tell a tale.

Neet-Fo.

I.

TH' wynt blows keen through th'
shiverin' thorns,
An' th' leet[1] looks wild i'th sky;
Come, Tet, stir up that fire; an' draw
That keyther[2] gently by;
I've done my weshin', gronny; an'
I've tidied every thing,
An', neaw I'll sit me deawn to sew,
An' hearken th' kettle sing.

II.

Bring in some coals; an' shut that dur,—
It's quite a wintry day;
Reitch deawn that ham: for Robin likes
A relish to his tay.[3]
Sweep th' grate; an' set yon table eawt;
Put th' tay-pot upo' th' oon;[1]
Its gettin' on for baggin'-time,[2]
An' he'll be comin' soon.

III.

The fire bruns[3] clear; an' th' heawse begins
A-lookin' brisk an' breet,
As th' time draws near when he gets back
Fro' teawn at th' edge o' neet;
It makes one hutch[4] wi' glee to yer
A favourite fuut come whoam;
An' it's very fine to hearken, when
One thinks it's sure to come.

IV.

Th' cat pricks up her ears at th' sneck,
  Wi' mony a leetsome toot;
An' th' owd arm-cheer i'th corner seems
  As if it yerd his fuut;
Th' window blinks; an' th' clock begins
  A-tickin' leawd an' fain;
An' th' tin things winkin' upo' th' wole,—
  They groon as breet again.

V.

Th' kettle's hummin' o'er wi' fun—
  Just look at th' end o'th speawt;
It's like a little sooty lad
  That's set his lips to sheawt:
Th' wayter-drops 'at fo'n fro' th' tap,
  Are gettin' wick wi' glee;
An' yo're fain, gronny, too,—I know,—
  But noan as fain as me!

VI.

Keep th' rockers gooin' soft and slow,
  An' shade that leet away;
I think this little duck's o'th mend,
  Hoo sleeps so weel to-day;
Doze on, my darlin'; keep 'em shut,—
  Those teeny[1] windows blue;
Good Lord; if aught should happen thee,
  What could thi mammy do!

VII.

Here, gronny, put this cover on,
  An' tuck it nicely in;
Keep th' keyther stirrin' gently; an'
  Make very little din:
An' lap thoose dimpled honds away
  Fro' th' frosty winter air;
They lie'n a-top o'th bit o' quilt,
  Like two clock-hommers theer!

---

[1] *Teeny*, tiny.

VIII.

But stop ; hoo's laughin' ! Come, hie up,—
  My bonny little puss !
God bless it ! Daddy's noan far off ;
  Let mammy have a buss !
He's here ! He's here ! Tet, bring that cheer !
  Eh, dear ; these darlin's two !
If it wur not for this chylt an' him
  What could a body do !

A Lift on the Way.

I.

COME, what's th' use o' fratchin',[1] lads, this life's noan so lung,
So, if yo'n gether reawnd, aw'll try my hond at a sung;
It may shew a guidin' glimmer to some wand'rer astray,
Or, haply, gi' some poor owd soul a lift on the way:
A lift on the way;
A lift on the way;
Or, haply, gi' some poor owd soul a lift on the way.

II.

Life's road's full o' ruts; it's very slutchy[2] an' it's dree;[3]
An' mony a worn-eawt limper lies him deawn there to dee;
Then, fleawnd'rin low i'th gutter, he looks reawnd wi' dismay,
To see if aught i'th world can give a lift on the way:
A lift on the way;
A lift on the way;
To see if aught i'th world can give a lift on the way.

III.

There's some folk 'at mun trudge it, an' there's some folk 'at may ride,
But, never mortal mon con tell what chance may betide;
To-day, he may be blossomin', like roses i' May;
To-morn, he may be beggin' for a lift on the way:
A lift on the way;
A lift on the way;
To-morn, he may be beggin' for a lift on the way.

---

[1] *Fratchin'*, quarrelling.

[2] *Slutchy*, miry. [3] *Dree*, wearily-continuous.

IV.

Good-will, it's a jewel, where there's little else to spare;
An' a mon may help another though his pouch may be bare;
A gen'rous heart, like sunshine, brings good cheer in its ray
An' a friendly word can sometimes give a lift on the way:
A lift on the way;
A lift on the way;
An' a friendly word can sometimes give a lift on the way.

V.

Like posies that are parchin' in the midsummer sun,
There's mony a poor heart faints afore the journey be run;
Let's lay the dust wi' kindness, till the close of the day,
An' gi' these droopin' travellers a lift on the way:
A lift on the way;
A lift on the way;
An' gi' these droopin' travellers a lift on the way.

VI.

Oh, soft be his pillow, when he sinks deawn to his rest,
That can keep the lamp o' charity alive in his breast;
May pleasant feelin's haunt him as he's dozin' away,
An' angels give him, up aboon,[1] a lift on the way:
A lift on the way;
A lift on the way;
An' angels give him, up aboon, a lift on the way.

VII.

Jog on, my noble comrades, then; an'—so mote it be,—[2]
That hond in hond we travel till the day that we dee;
An' neaw, to end my ditty, lads, let's heartily pray
That heaven may give us ev'ry one a lift on the way!
A lift on the way;
A lift on the way;
That heaven may give us ev'ry one a lift on the way!

---

[1] *Aboon*, above.

[2] *So mote it be*, so might it be.

Yesterneet.

I.

I GEET up a-milkin' this mornin',—
I geet up afore it wur leet;
I ne'er slept a minute for thinkin'
What Robin said yesterneet;
I've brokken two basins i'th dairy;
I've scoaded my gronny wi' tay;
It's no use o' tryin' a-spinnin'—
My wheel's eawt o' trim to-day.

CHORUS.

It's oh, yon Robin, yon Robin;
His e'en ne'er twinkle't so breet,
As they did when he meazur't my finger
For th' little gowd ring last neet!

II.

Eawr Dorothy's singin' i'th shippon;[1]
Eawr Jonathan's leawngin' i'th fowd;[2]
Eawr Tummy's at th' fair, where he lippens[3]
O' swappin' his cowt for gowd;[4]
My gronny's asleep wi' her knittin',
An' th' kittlin's playing with th' yarn;
Eawr Betty's gone eawt wi' a gallon
To th' chaps at their wark i'th barn.

CHORUS.—But oh, yon Robin, yon Robin.

III.

Th' lasses an' lads are i'th meadow ;
  They're gettin' their baggin'[5] i'th hay ;
I yer 'em as leetsome as layrocks,[6]
  I'th sky on a shiny day ;
But, little care I for their marlocks ;[7]
  I dunnot want folk to see,
Though I'm fitter for cryin' than laughin',
  There's nob'dy as fain as me.

CHORUS.—For oh, yon Robin, yon Robin.

IV.

When I crept into th' nook wi' my sewin',
  My mother peeped reawnd so sly ;
Hoo know'd I wur glentin' at th' coppice,
  Where Robin comes ridin' by ;
Then hoo coom to me, snurchin' an' tootin',
  An' whisperin', " Heaw dost feel ?
Dost think I should send for a doctor ? "
  But, th' doctor hoo knows reet weel.

CHORUS.—It's oh, yon Robin, yon Robin.

V.

My feyther sits dozin' i'th corner,—
  He's dreamin' o'th harvest day :
When Robin comes in for his daughter,—
  Eh, what'll my feyther say !
Th' rosebuds are peepin' i'th garden :
  An' th' blossom's o'th apple tree ;
Oh, heaw will life's winter time find us,—
  Yon Robin o' mine, an' me !

CHORUS.—Oh, yon Robin, yon Robin !

VI.

Then, hey for kisses an' blushes,
An' hurryin' to an' fro;
An' hey for sly, sweet whispers,
That nob'dy but me mun know!

Then, hey for rings, an' for ribbins,
An' bonnets, an' posies fine!
An' eh,—it's o' in a flutter,—
This little fond heart o' mine!

CHORUS.—For oh, yon Robin, yon Robin;
His e'en ne'er twinkle't so breet,
As they did when he meazur't my finger
For th' little gowd ring last neet!

I've Worn My Bits o' Shoon Away.

I.

I'VE worn my bits o' shoon[1] away,
Wi' roving up an' deawn,
To see yon moorlan' valleys, an'
Yon little country teawn:
The dule tak' shoon, an' stockin's too!
My heart feels hutchin'-fain;
An', if I trudge it bar-fuut,[2] lads,
I'll see yon teawn again!

II.

It's what care I for cities grand,—
We never shall agree;
I'd rayther live where th' layrock sings,—
A country teawn for me!
A country teawn, where one can meet
Wi' friends an' neighbours known;
Where one can lounge i'th' market-place,
An' see the meadows mown.

---

[1] *Shoon*, shoes. [2] *Bar-fuut*, bare-foot.

III.

Yon moorland hills are bloomin' wild
  At th' endin' o' July;
Yon woodlan' cloofs, an' valleys green,—
  The sweetest under th' sky;
Yon dainty rindles,[2] dancin' deawn
  Fro' th' meawntains into th' plain;—
As soon as th' new moon rises, lads,
  I'm off to th' moors again!

IV.

There's hearty lads among yon hills,
  An' in yon country teawn;
They'n far moor sense than prouder folk,—[3]
  I'll uphowd it for a creawn;
They're wick an' warm at wark an' fun,[1]
  Wherever they may go,—
The primest breed o' lads i'th world,—
  Good luck attend 'em o'!

V.

Last neet I laft the city thrung,[2]
  An' climbed yon hillock green;
An' turned my face to th' moorlan' hills,
  Wi' th' wayter i' my e'en;[3]
Wi' th' wayter wellin' i' my e'en;—
  I'll bundle up, an' go,
An' I'll live an' dee i' my own countrie,
  Where the moorlan' breezes blow!

---

[1] *Wick an' warm at wark an' fun,* lively and earnest at work and fun.
[2] *Last neet I laft the city thrung,* last night I left the city throng.
[3] *Wi'th wayter i' my e'en,* with the water in mine eyes.

Gentle Jone.

I.

I SEE'D a thowtful[1] chap one day,
His face were mild, his toppin'[2] gray!
Wi' wanderin' fuut he went astray,
Deawn yon lone:[3]
I axed a lame owd mon i'th road,
To tell me what that chap were co'd;[4]
Says he, "I thowt oitch body[5] knowed
Gentle Jone!"

II.

"Owd lad," said I, "just look heaw ronk[6]
These daisies groo'n at th' edge o'th bonk;[7]
Let's keawer us deawn, an' have a conk,—[8]
Just till noon."

He poo'd a reech o' bacco eawt,
An' cheese an' moufin in a cleawt;
An' then began to tell abeawt
Gentle Jone!

---

[1] *I see'd a thowtful*, I saw a thoughtful.
[2] *Toppin'*, the hair on the front of the head.
[3] *Lone*, lane.
[4] *Co'd*, called,
[5] *Oitch body*, each body, each person.
[6] *Ronk*, rank, abundant.
[7] *Bonk*, a bank of land, a gentle slope,
[8] *Conk*, a chat.

III.

Says he, "Some folk o' brass are fond;
They're cowd i'th heart, an' crampt i'th hond;
But yon's the fleawer of o' this lond,—
Gentle Jone!
His heart's as true as guinea-gowd;
He's good to folk at's ill an' owd;
Childer poo'n his lap i'th fowd,—
Gentle Jone!

IV.

"I'll bet a creawn he's off to th' vale,
To yer some crayter's soory tale;
I never knowed his kindness fail,—
Gentle Jone!
O'er hill, an' cloof, an' moss, an' moor,
He's reet weel[2] known to folk at's poor;
A welcome fuut at every door,—
Gentle Jone!

V.

"He taks delight i' roving round.
To quiet nooks where sorrow's found;
He comes like rain to drufty ground,—
Gentle Jone!
He's very slow at thinkin' ill;
He'll pass a faut wi' reet good will;
An' doin' good's his pastime still,—
Gentle Jone!

VI.

An' when I broke this poor owd limb,
I should ha' dee'd except for him."
He said no moor; his e'en geet dim,—
Mine were th' same:
"Owd brid," said I, "let's have a gill!"

" Nawe, nawe," said he, " I'm noan so weel ;
It's time to paddle deawn this hill,
To th' owd dame."

VII.

'Twere nearly noon, i'th month o' May ;
We said we'd meet another day ;
An' then th' owd crayter limped away
Deawn th' green lone.
An' neaw, let's do the thing that's reet,
An' then, when death puts eawt er leet,[1]
We's haply ston a chance to meet
Gentle Jone !

---

[1] *Puts eawt er leet,* puts out our light.

Tum Rindle.

I.

TUM Rindle lope fro' the chimbley nook,
As th' winter sun wur sinkin':
I'm tired o' keawrin' here i'th smooke,
An' wastin' time i' thinkin':
It frets my heart, an' racks my broo—
It sets my yed a-stewin':
A man that wouldn't dee a foo,
Mun up, an' start a-doin'!

II.

Then, Mally, reitch my Sunday shoon,
To rom my bits o' toes in;
An' hond mo th' jug, fro' top o'th oon,—
An' let mo dip my nose in!
An', come, an' fill it up again;
An' dunnot look so deawldy;
There's nought can lick a marlock, when
One's brains are gettin' meawldy.

III.

Aw'll laithe a rook o' neighbour lads,—
Frisky cowts, an' bowd uns;
An' let 'em bring their mams an' dads;
We'n have it pranked wi' owd uns!
An' th' lads an' lasses they sha'n sing,
An' fuut it, leet an' limber;
An' Robin Lilter, he shall bring
His merry bit o' timber!

IV.

An' Joe shall come, an' Jone, an' Ben ;
  An' poor owd limpin' 'Lijah ;
An' Mall, an' Sall, an' Fan, an' Nan,
  An' curly-pated 'Bijah ;
An' gentle Charlie shall be theer ;
  An' little Dick, the ringer ;
An' Moston Sam,—aw like to yer
  A snowy-yedded singer !

V.

I'll poo mi gronny eawt o'th' nook,
  An' send for Dolly Maybo',
For, when hoo's gradely donned, hoo'll look
  As grand as th' queen o' Shayba ;
An' little Nell shall doance[1] wi' me,—
  Eawr Nelly's yung an' bonny ;
An' when aw've had a doance wi' thee,
  Aw'll caper wi' my gronny !

VI.

Then, Mally, fill it up again ;
  An' dunnot look so deawldy ;
There's nought can lick a marlock, when
  One's brains are gettin' meawldy !
We're young an' hearty ; dunnot croak,
  Let's frisk it neaw, or never ;
So, here's good luck to country folk,
  An' country fun, for ever !

[1] *Doance*, dance.

Bonny Nan.

I.

HEIGH, Ned, owd mon, I feel as fain
As th' breetest brid 'at sings i' May;
Come, sit tho deawn; I'll wear a creawn;
We'n have a roozin rant to-day!
Let's doance an' sing; I've bought a ring
For bonny Nan i'th Owler dale;
Then heigh for fun; my mopin's done!
An' neaw I'm brisk as bottle't ale!
Oh, guess, owd brid,
What's beawn to be;
For I like Nan,—
An' hoo likes me!

II.

Twelve months at after Robin dee'd,
Hoo look'd so deawn, wi' ne'er a smile;
I couldn't find i' heart or mind
To cheep o' weddin' for a while;
I thought I'd bide; but still I sighed
For th' mournin' cleawd to clear away;
I watched her e'en groo breet again,—
A layrock tootin' eawt for day!
Then, guess, owd brid,
What's beawn to be;
For I like Nan,—
An' hoo likes me!

III.

My Nanny's fair, an' trim, an' rare;
A modest lass, an' sweet to see;
Her e'en are blue, her heart it's true,—
An' Nanny's hardly twenty-three;
An' life's so strung, when folk are yung;
That waitin' lunger wouldno do;
These moor-end lads, hoo turns their yeds,—
Hoo's bin a widow lung enoo!

Then guess, owd brid,
What's beawn to be;
For I like Nan,—
An' hoo likes me!

IV.

I've sin, at neet, abeawt a leet,[1]
A midge keep buzzin' to an' fro,
Then dart at th' shine, 'at looked so fine,
And brun his wings at th' end of o';[2]
That midge's me, its plain to see,—
My wings are brunt, an' yet, I'm fain;
For, wheer I leet,[3] I find so sweet,
I's never want to fly again!

Then guess, owd brid,
What's beawn to be;
For I like Nan,—
An' hoo likes me!

---

[1] *At neet abeawt a leet*, at night about a light.

[2] *An brun his wings at th' end ov o*, and burn his wings at the en of all.

[3] *Leet*, ali ht, drop upon.

Tickle Times.

I.

HERES' Robin looks fearfully gloomy,
An' Jamie keeps starin' at th' greawnd,
He's thinkin o' th' table at's empty,
An th' little things yammerin'[1] reawnd ;
It looks very dark just afore us,—
But, keep your hearts eawt o' your shoon,—[2]
Though clouds may be thickenin' o'er us,
There's lots o' blue heaven aboon !

II.

But, when a mon's honestly willin',
An' never a stroke to be had,
And clemmin'[3] for want ov a shillin',—
No wonder that he should be sad ;
It troubles his heart to keep seein'
His little brids[1] feedin' o'th air ;
An' it feels very hard to be deein',[2]
An' never a mortal to care.

III.

But life's sich a quare[3] bit o' travel,—
A marlock[4] wi' sun an' wi' shade,—
An' then, on a bowster[5] o' gravel,
They lay'n us i' bed wi' a spade ;
It's no use a peawtin an' fratchin'—[6]
As th' whirligig 's twirlin' areawnd,
Have at it again ; an' keep scratchin'
As lung as yor yed 's above greawnd.

IV.

Iv one could but grope i'th inside on't,
  There's trouble i' every heart ;
An' thoose that 'n th' biggest o'th pride on't,
  Oft leeten· o'th keenest o'th smart.
Whatever may chance to come to us,
  Let's patiently hondle er share,—
For there's mony a fine suit o' clooas,
  That covers a murderin' care.

V.

There's danger i' every station,—
  I'th palace as much as i'th cot ;
There's hanker[1] i' every condition,
  An' canker[2] i' every lot ;
There's folk that are weary o' livin',
  That never fear't hunger nor cowd ;
An there's mony a miserly craiter,[3]
  That's deed ov a surfeit o' gowd.

VI.

One feels, neaw at times are so nippin',
  A mon's at a troublesome schoo',
That slaves like a horse for a livin',
  An flings it away like a foo ;
But, as pleasur 's sometimes a misfortin',
  An' trouble sometimes a good thing,—
Though we livin' o'th floor same as layrocks,[4]
We'n go up, like layrocks, to sing !

---

[1] *Hanker*, to fret for, to long for something.
[2] *Canker*, a sore place, dissatisfaction.
[3] *Craiter*, creature.
[4] *Layrocks*, larks.

Jamie's Frolic.

I.

ONE neet aw crope whoam when my weighvin' were
o'er,
To brush mo, an' wesh mo, an' fettle my yure [1]
Then, trailin' abeawt, wi' my heart i' my shoon,
Kept tryin' my hond at a bit of a tune,
As Mally sit rockin',
An' darnin' a stockin',
An' tentin'[2] her bakin' i'th o'on.

II.

Th' chylt were asleep, an' my clooas were reet,
Th' baggin'[3] were ready, an' o' lookin' sweet;
But, aw're mazy, an' nattle,[4] an' fasten't to tell
What the dule it could be that're ailin' mysel';
An' it made me so naught,
That, o' someheaw, aw thought,
"Aw could just like a snap at eawr Mall."

III.

Poor lass, hoo were kinder becose aw were quare;
"Come, Jamie, an' sattle thisel'[1] in a cheer;
Thae's looked very yonderly[2] mony a day;
It's grievin' to see heaw thae'rt wearin' away,
An' trailin' abeawt,
Like a hen at's i'th meawt;[3]
Do, pritho, poo up to thi tay!

---

[1] *Fettle my yure*, put my hair to rights.
[2] *Tentin'*, minding, taking care of.
[3] *Baggin'*, the afternoon meal.
[4] *Nattle*, snappish, short-tempered.

IV.

"Thae wants some new flannels,—thae's getten a cowd,—
Thae'rt noather so ugly, my lad, nor so owd,—
But, thae'rt makin' thysel' into nought but a slave,
Wi' weighvin', an' thinkin', an' tryin' to save ;—
Get summat to heyt,[4]
Or thae'll go eawt o' seet,—
For thae'rt wortchin'[5] thisel' into th' grave."

V.

Thinks I, "Th' lass 's reet, an aw houd with her wit ;"
So, aw said,—for aw wanted to cheer her a bit,—
"Owd crayter, aw've noan made my mind up to dee,—
A frolick 'll just be the physic for me !
Aw'll see some fresh places,
An' look at fresh faces,—
An' go have a bit ov a spree !"

VI.

Then, bumpin' an' splashin' her kettle went deawn ;
"I'th name o' good Katty, Jem, wheer arto beawn ?
An' what sort o' faces dost want,—con to tell ?
Aw deawt thae'rt for makin' a foo o' thisel',—
The dule may tent th' oon ;
Iv aw go witheawt shoon,
Aw'll see where thae gwos to, mysel' !"

VII.

Thinks I, "Th' fat's i'th fire,—aw mun make it no wur,—
For there's plenty o' feightin' to do eawt o'th dur,—
So, aw'll talk very prattily to her, as heaw,
Or else hoo'll have houd o' my toppin in neaw ;
An' bith leet in her e'en,
It were fair to be seen
That hoo're ready to rive me i' teaw.

---

1 *Sattle thisel'*, settle thyself.
2 *Yonderly*, absent-minded, thinking far away.
3 *I'th meawt*, in the moult, moulting.
4 *Get summat to heyt*, get somewhat to eat.
5 *Wortchin'*, working.

VIII.

Iv truth mun be towd, aw began to be fain
To study a bit o' my cwortin' again;
So aw said to her, "Mally, this world's rough enoo!
To fo' eawt wi' thoose one likes best, winnut do,—
It's a very sore smart,
An' it sticks long i' th heart,"—
An', egad, aw said nought but what's true!

IX.

Lord, heaw a mon talks when his heart's in his tung!
Aw roos't her,[1] poor lass, an' showed hoo wur wrung,
Till hoo took mo bith hond, with a tear in her e'e,
An' said, "Jamie, there's nob'dy as tender as thee!
Forgi mo, lad, do;
For aw'm nobbut a foo,—
An' bide wi' me, neaw, till aw dee!"

X.

So, we'n bide one another, whatever may come;
For, there's no peace i'th world if there's no peace a-whoam;
An' neaw, when a random word gi's her some pain,
Or makes her a little bit cross in her grain,
Sunshine comes back,
As soon as aw crack
O' beginning my cwortin' again.

---

[1] *Aw roos't her*, I praised her.

Owd Pinder.

I.

OWD Pinder were a rackless[1] foo,
An' spent his days i' spreein';
At th' end of every drinkin-do,
He're sure to crack o' deein';[2]
"Go, sell my rags, an' sell my shoon;
Aw's never live to trail 'em;
My ballis-pipes[3] are eawt o' tune,
An' th' wynt[4] begins to fail 'em!"

II.

"Eawr Matty's very fresh an' yung;—
'Twould any mon bewilder;—
Hoo'll wed again afore its lung,
For th' lass is fond o' childer;

My bit o' brass 'll fly,—yo'n see,—
When th' coffin-lid has screened me,—
It gwos again my pluck to dee,
An' lev her wick beheend me."

---

[1] *Rackless*, reckless.
[2] *Crack o' deein'*, hint at dying.
[3] *Ballis-pipes*, bellows-pipes, lungs.
[4] *Th' wynt*, the wind, the breath.

III.

" Come, Matty, come, an' cool my yed ;
  Aw'm finish'd, to my thinkin' ;"
Hoo happed him nicely up, an' said,
  " Thae's brought it on wi' drinkin' ; "—
" Nay, nay," said he, " my fuddle's done ;
  We're partin' tone fro tother ;
So, promise me that when aw'm gwon,
  Thae'll never wed another ! "

IV.

" Th' owd tale," said hoo, an' laft her stoo ;
  " Its rayly past believin' ;
Thee think o'th world thea'rt goin' to,
  An' lev this world to th' livin' ;
What use to me can deeod folk be ?
  Thae's kilt thisel' wi' spreein' ;
An' if that's o' thae wants wi' me,
  Get forrud wi' thi deein' ! "

V.

He scrat his yed, he rubbed his e'e,
  An' then he donned his breeches ;
" Eawr Matty gets as fause,"[1] said he,
  " As one o' Pendle witches ;[2]
If ever aw'm to muster wit,
  It mun be now or never ;
Aw think aw'll try to live a bit ;
  It would'nt do to lev her ! "

---

[1] *Fause*, cunning.

[2] *Pendle witches*, Pendle Forest was notoriously associated with the old witch superstitions of Lancashire.

Th' Goblin Parson.

I.

TH' wynt wur still i'th shade o'th hill,
An' stars began o' glowin',
I'th fadin' leet, one summer neet,
When th' dew wur softly foin';
Wi' weary shanks, by primrose banks,
Where rindlin' weet[1] wur shinin',
Aw whistle't careless, wanderin' slow,
Toward my cot inclinin'.

II.

Through th' woodlan' green aw tooted[2] keen,
For th' little window winkin';—
Th' stars may shine, they're noan as fine
As Matty's candle blinkin';
O'er th' rosy hedge aw went to th' ridge
O'th lonesome-shaded plantin',[3]
To get another blink o'th leet
That set my heart a-pantin'.

III.

Then deawn bi'th well i'th fairy-dell,
Wi' trees aboon it knittin',
Where, near an' fur, ther nowt astir
But bats i'th eawl-leet[1] flittin';
An' feeorfu' seawnds that rustle't reawnd
I' mony a goblin-flitter,
As swarmin' dark to flaysome wark[2]
They flew wi' fiendish titter.

IV.

Theer, reet anent, aw geet a glent[3]
That brought a shiver o'er me,
For, fair, i'th track ther summat black
Coom creepin' on afore me;
It wur not clear,—but it wur theer,—
Wi' th' gloomy shadow blendin',
Neaw black an' slim, neaw grey an' grim,
Wi' noather side nor endin'.

V.

Cowd drops wur tremblin' o' my broo,
As there aw stoode belated;—[4]
Aw durstn't turn,—aw durstn't goo,—
But shut my e'en, an' waited;
An' just as aw begun to pray,
There coom fro' th' creepin' spectre
A weel known voice, that said, "Well, James!"—
'Twur nowt but th' village rector.

VI.

"Well, James," said he, "I'm fain to see
Your pew so weel attended,
But then, yo shouldn't fo' asleep
Afore my sarmon's ended;
To dreawsy ears it 's useless quite
To scatter holy teychin';[1]
Why don't yo bring a bit o' snuff,
An' tak it while I'm preychin'?"[2]

VII.

"Well, well," said aw, "there's mony a way
O' keepin' e'en fro closin',
A needle would keep th' body wake,
An' th' soul might still be dozin':—

But this receipt would set it reet,
If th' mixture wur a warm un,—
Yo' get some stingin' gospel-snuff,
An' put it into th' sarmon."

VIII.

He stare't like mad, but th' good owd lad
Then grip't my hond, warm-hearted,
An' said, "Yo're reet, yo're reet—good neet!"
An' that wur heaw we parted.
It touched my heart, an' made it smart,
He spoke so mild and pratty;—
Aw blest him as he walked away,
An' then went whoam to Matty.

Come, Jamie, let's Undo thi Shoon.

I.

Come, Jamie, let's undo thi shoon; ;
An' don summat dry o' thi feet ;
Wi' toilin' i'th sheaw'r up an' deawn ;
Aw'm fleyed at thi stockin's are weet ;
An', here, wi' my yung uns i'th neest,
Aw bin heark'nin' to th' patter o'th rain,
An' longing for th' wanderin' brid
To comfort my spirits again.

II.

To-day, when it pelted at th' height,
"Aw'll ston it no longer," said I ;
For, rayly, it didn't look reet
To keawer under cover so dry ;
So, though it were rainin' like mad,
Aw thought,—for my heart gav a swell,—
"Come deawn asto will, but yon lad
Shall not have it o' to his-sel' !"

III.

So, whippin' my bucket i'th rain,
Aw ga' th' bits o' windows a swill ;
An', though aw geet drenched to my skin,
Aw 're better content wi' mysel' ;
But, theaw stons theer smilin' o'th floor,
Like a sun-fleawer drippin' wi' weet ;
Eh, Jamie, theaw knowsn't, awm sure,
Heaw fain aw'm to see tho to-neet !

IV.

Eh, lass, what's a sheawer to me?
  Aw've plenty o' sun in my breast,
Mi wark keeps me hearty an' free,
  An' gi's me a relish for rest;
Aw'm noan made o' sugar nor saut,
  That melts wi' a steepin' o' rain;
An', as for my jacket,—it's nought,—
  Aw'll dry it by th' leet o' thi e'en! [1]

V.

Come, sit tho down close by my side,—
  Aw'm full as a cricket wi' glee;
Aw'm trouble't wi' nothin' but pride,
  An' o' on it owing to thee;
Theaw trim little pattern for wives;—
  Come, give a poor body a kiss!
Aw wish every storm of our lives
  May end up as nicely as this!

---

[1] *Th' leet o' thi e'en*, the light of thine eyes.

While takin' a Wift o' my Pipe.

I.

WHILE takin' a wift o' my pipe, tother neet
A thowt trickled into my pate,
That sulkin' becose everything isn't sweet,
Is nobbut a foolish consate;
If mon had bin made for a bit of a spree,
An' th' world were a marlockin' schoo',
Wi' nought nobbut heytin', an' drinkin', an' glee,
An' haliday gam to go through,
He'd sicken afore
His frolic were o'er,
An' feel he'd bin born for a foo.

II.

Poor crayter, he's o' discontentment an' deawt,
Whatever his fortin may be;
He's just like a choilt at goes cryin' abeawt,
"Eawr Johnny's moor traycle nor me;"
One minute he's trouble't, next minute he's fain,
An' then, they're so blended i' one,
It's hard to tell whether he's laughin' through pain,
Or whether he's peawtin' for fun;—
He stumbles, an' grumbles,
He struggles, an' juggles,—
He capers a bit,—an' he's gone.

III.

It's wise to be humble i' prosperous ways,
For trouble may chance to be nee ,
It's wise for to struggle wi' sorrowful days,
Till sorrow breeds sensible glee;
He's rich that, contented wi' little, lives weel,
An' nurses that little to moor;
He's weel off at's rich, if he nobbut can feel
He's brother to thoose that are poor;
An' to him 'at does fair,
Though his livin' be bare,
Some comfort shall ever be sure.

IV.

We'n nobbut a lifetime a-piece here below,
An' th' lungest is very soon spent;
There's summat aboon measur's cuts[1] for us o',
An' th' most on 'em nobbut a fent;[2]
Lung or short, rough or fine, little matter for that,
We'n make th' best o'th stuff till it's done,
An' when it leets eawt to get rivven[3] a bit,
Let's darn it as weel as we con;
When th' order comes to us
To doff these old clooas,[4]
There'll surely be new uns to don.

---

[1] *Cuts*, a name for a weaver's piece, or web of cloth.
[2] *Fent*, a part or fragment of the web of cloth.
[3] *Rivven*, torn. [4] *Clooas*, clothes.

God Bless Thi Silver Yure.

I.

HONE, lad, though thi hond's
Like reawsty iron to feel,
There's very few i'th lond
Aw like to gripe as weel.
Tha'll never dee i'th dumps
Becose o' bein' poor,
Thae good owd king o' trumps,—
God bless thi silver yure !

II.

Poo up to th' side o'th hob,
An' rest thi weary shanks,
An' dunnot fret thi nob
Wi' fortin an' her pranks;
These folk at's preawd an' rich
May tremble at her freawn ;—
They'n further far nor sich
As thee to tumble deawn.

III.

Theaw never longs for wine,
Nor dainties rich an' rare,
For sich a life as thine
Can sweeten simple fare ;
Contented wi' thi meal,
Thae 's wit enough to know
That daisies liven weel
Where tulips connot grow.

IV.

An' though thi clooas[2] are rough,
  An' gettin' very owd,
They'n onswer weel enough
  To keep thi limbs fro' cowd;
A foo would pine away
  I' sich a suit as thine,
But, thaer't the stuff to may
  A fustian jacket fine.

V.

A tattered clout may lap
  A very noble prize;
A king may be, by hap,
  A beggar i' disguise.
When tone has laft his feast,
  An' tother done his crust,[1]
Then, which is which, at last,—
  These little piles o' dust?

VI.

An' though thy share o' life,
  May seem a losin' game,
Thae's striven fair i'th strife,
  An' kept a dacent aim;
No meawse-nooks[2] i' thi mind,
  Nor malice i' thi breast,
Thae's still bin true an' kind,
  An' trusted fate wi' th' rest.

VII.

Through trouble, toil, an' wrung,
  Thae's whistle't at thi wark,
Thae's wrostle't life so lung,
  Thi limbs are gettin' stark;
But sich a heart as thine 's

A never failin' friend;
It cheers a mon's decline,
An' keeps it sweet to th' end.

VIII.

Thy banner 'll soon be furled,
An' then they'n ha' to tell,
"He travelled th' dirty world,
An' never soil't his-sel'!"
An' when aw come to dee,
An' death has taen his tow,[1]
Aw hope to leet[2] o' thee,—
God bless thy snowy pow![3]

---

[1] *Tow*, toll.
[2] *Leet*, to alight upon, to meet with.
[3] *Pow*, poll.

Margit's Comin'.

I.

EH! Sam, whatever doesto meeon?
Aw see thae 'rt theer i'th nook again,—
Where aw 've a gill thae's nine or ten;
Hast dropt into a fortin?
Aw wonder heaw a mon can sit
An' waste his bit o' wage an' wit:
Iv aw're thi wife, aw'd make tho flit,—
Wi' little time to start in.

II.

But, houd; yo'r Margit's up i'th teawn;
Aw yerd her ax for thee at th' Crown;
An' just meet neaw, aw scamper't deawn;—
It's true as aught i'th Bible!
Thae knows yo'r Margit weel, of owd;
Her tung,—it makes mo fair go cowd,
Sin' th' day hoo broke my nose i'th fowd
Wi' th' edge o'th porritch thible.

III.

It 's ten to one hoo 'll[1] co' in here,
An' poo[2] tho eawt o'th corner cheer;
So, sit fur[3] back, where th' runnin's clear;—
Aw 'll keep my een o'th window;
Thae'm[4] mind thi hits, an' when aw sheawt,
Be limber-legged,[5] an' lammas[6] eawt;
An', though hoo 'll not believe, aw deawt,
Aw 'll swear aw never sin tho.

---

[1] *Hoo 'll*, she'll, she will.
[2] *Poo*, pull.
[3] *Fur*, further.
[4] *Thae'm*, thou must.
[5] *Limber-legged*, nimble-legged.
[6] *Lammas*, to run away.

IV.

Aw 'll bite my tung, aw will, bith mon;
Aw 'll plug my ears up, till hoo 's gone;
A grooin' tree could hardly ston
A savage woman flytin';
If folk were nobbut o' i'th mind
To make their bits o' booses kind,
There 'd be less wanderin' eawt to find
A corner to be quiet in.

V.

It 's nearly three o'clock bith chime:
This ale o' Jem's is very prime;
Aw 'll keawer mo deawn till baggin-time,[1]
An' have a reech[2] o' bacco;
Aw guess thae's yerd o' Clinker lad[3]
An' Liltin' Jenny gettin wed;[4]
An' Collop gooin' wrang i'th yed,—[5]
But, that's nought mich to crack o'.[6]

VI.

There's news that chaps 'at wore a creawn,
Are getting powler't[7] up an' deawn
They're puncin'[8] 'em fro teawn to teawn,
Like foot-bo's in a pastur;[9]

---

[1] *Aw 'll keawer mo deawn till baggin' time*, I will sit me down till the afternoon meal-time.

[2] *Reech*, a smoke.

[3] *Thae's yerd o' Clinker lad*, thou hast heard of Clinker's lad.

[4] *Gettin wed*, getting married.

[5] *Wrang i'th yed*, wrong in the head, crazy.

[6] *That's not mich to crack o'*, that's not much to talk of, or to wonder at.

[7] *Powler't*, jolted, knocked to and fro.

[8] *Puncin'*, kicking.

[9] *Like foot-bo's in a pastur'*, like footballs in a field.

Yon Garibaldi's gan 'em silk ;[1]
Th' owd lad ; he's fairly made 'em swilk ;[2]
An' neaw, they sen he's sellin' milk[3]
  To raise new clooas for Ayster.[4]

VII.

There's some are creepin' eawt o'th slutch,[5]
An' some are gettin' deawn i'th doitch ;[6]
Bith mon,[7] aw never yerd of sich
  A world for change o' fortin' !
They're gooin' groaning eawt o'th seet,
They're comin' cryin' into th' leet ;
But, howd ! aw yeard, o' Monday neet,
  A tale abeawt a cwortin'.[8]

VIII.

Poo up ![1] aw'll tell it iv aw con ;—
Thae knows that little bow-legged mon,
But, heigh,—owd lad ! yo'r Margit's yon,—
  Hoo's comin' like a racer !—
Some foo[2] has put her upo' th' track ;
Cut, Sam ; hoo'll have us in a crack !
Aw said hoo'd come,—let's run eawt th' back ;
  Bith mass,[3] aw dar not face her !

---

[1] *Gan 'em silk*, given them silk, thrashed them finely, thoroughly.

[2] *Swilk*, to make a noise inside, like a half-filled barrel, when shaken.

[3] *He's sellin' milk*, an allusion to Garibaldi's farming in the island of Caprera.

[4] *To raise new clcoas for Ayster*, to raise new clothes for Easter. Country people in Lancashire generally make a superstitious struggle to wear some kind of new clothing on Easter Sunday.

[5] *Slutch*, mire.

[6] *Doitch*, ditch.

[7] *Bith mon*, by the man, an ancient allusion to the Saviour of mankind.

[8] *Cwortin'*, courting.

Hard Weather.

WINTER, 1878-9.

I.

GOOD lorjus days, what times are these,
For clemmin' an' for cowd;
For doleful looks, an' wintry nooks,
Where folk are poor an' owd;
For hopeless care an' dark despair,
An' gloomy want o' trust;
For fireless hearths, an' cupboards bare,
An' bitter want o' crust.
But, bide lads, bide,
For a happier tide;
An' keep yor hearts out o' yor shoon;
Through thick an' thin,
We'n ne'er give in:
There's a bit o' blue sky aboon!

II.

There never wur sich mournful cries
O' famine yerd afore;
John Chinaman's bin clemmed to death,
An' India's suffered sore;
Yor mills may weel be stonnin' still,
Yor markets weel be slack;
For when folk's nipt for want o' meight,
They'n nought to spare for th' back.
CHORUS—But, bide lads, etc.

III.

Sich strikes, an' rows, an' breakages,
There never yet wur known;
Sich frettin', an' sich chettin', an'
Sich bitter starvin' moan;
These knavish pranks i' trusted banks
Are spreadin' ruin round;
An' every hour, the tradin' ranks
Are crashin' to the ground.
CHORUS—But, bide lads, etc.

IV.

Whilst trade declines, an' taxes rise,
And ruin stalks the land,
We groan to see the good we prize,
Crushed by a rampant band;
'Tis ours to watch each bloody fray
And mad gunpowder plot;
And, win the day whoever may,
'Tis ours to pay the shot.
CHORUS—But, bide lads, etc.

V.

Though th' bitter air, an' livin' bare,
Gets keener every day;
An' th' emptier folks' pockets are,
The more they han to pay;
Though strikes, an' wars, an' swindlin' tricks
Are sendin' th' wide world wrong;
Yet, come what will, this shall be still
The burden of my song,—
CHORUS—Bide, lads, bide, etc.

Come, Limber Lads.

I.

COME, limber[1] lads, so leet an' gay,
Aw'm fain we're wick an' hearty;
To-neet we'n have a haliday—
To-morn we's find it warty:[2]
Like sailors, thrut[3] bith stormy main
Into a nook together,—
One hour o' friendly fun, an' then,
Again for wind and weather.

II.

Owd Time,—though, when a mon's i'th dumps,
He's seldom in a hurry,—
Nips up his shins, an' off he stumps,
The minute one gets merry;
Life's road,—though not as dree[4] as his,—
It's harder wark to travel;
One leets o' few sich nooks as this,
An' th' journey ends i'th gravel.

III.

Then clink and sing, my lucky lads,
An' frisk it while yo're able;
There's cheepin' layrocks round the board,
An' plenty upo' th' table.
Come, crack yo'r jokes, an' let 'em leet,
O sly deception scornin';
We'n prank it out wi' glee to-neet,
An' strike to wark i' th mornin'.

---

1 *Limber*, lithe, active.
2 *Warty*, wark-day, work-day.
3 *Thrut*, thrown.
4 *Dree*, wearily, continuous.

IV.

If o' that wanders under th' sky
  Be grass, that cannot linger,
Let every mortal blade that's dry
  Cock up his little finger.
Then, fill for him that's full o' fun,—
  An' let it be a thumper ;
An' th' lad that thinks he's nearly done,
  We'n rooze him wi' a bumper !

V.

An' now, to end this friendly rant,—
  Turn up yo'r tots[2] to th' ceilin' ;
Let's hope that he may ne'er feel scant
  That's never scant o' feeling !
Good luck to th' lad that wants a wife,
  Wi' rosy chens[3] to bind him !
An' th' mon that wants a foo,—bith life,—
  I' th' lookin'-glass he'll find him !

The Garland.

AIR—"*Cupid's Garden.*"

I.

TWAS when the dawn of mornin'
Began to stir i'th sky,
I donned mysel' to wander
Afore the dew wur dry;
To wander in the gay greenwood,
Reet early I did rove,—
I could not sleep upon my bed
For thinkin' of my love.

II.

Down in a bonny dingle,
Where sometimes we did stray,
Our vows of love to mingle,
At close of summer day;
It's there, where oft among her hair
The flowers of spring I've wove,
I sat me down to think upon
The girl that I do love.

III.

It's there I made a garlan',
My darlin' for to don,
And the posies that were in it,
They shinéd like the sun;
The dewy posies, wild and sweet,
All in the leafy grove;
It breaks my heart to think upon
The girl that I do love.

IV.

The cowslip, and the speedwell,
With a dewdrop in its e'e,—
An' the wild rose, an' the bluebell,
They blend so bonnilie ;
An' the honey-suckle, wand'rin wild,
With violets blue, I wove,
They made me for to think upon
The girl that I do love.

V.

An' when I poo'd my posies,
The small birds they did sing ;
An' when I wove my garlan',
They made the woods to ring ;
On every tree, the wild birds' glee,
Rang through the leafy grove,
As I came away, at dawn of day,
Still thinkin' of my love.

VI.

Oh, the mornin' sun it rises
To cheer my heart's delight,
An' the silver moon she wanders
Among the clouds at night ;
An' the twinklin' stars that look so fine,
All in the heavens above,—
At wark or play, by neet an' day,
I'm thinkin' of my love.

To Edwin Waugh,*

ON HIS SEVENTIETH BIRTHDAY, JANUARY 29TH, 1887.

I.

'TIS over thirty years, friend Waugh,
Since thou and I first met :
A manly face, a twinkling eye,
A voice to music set.

II.

Were thine to please, to charm, to win,
All round the social board,
Where kindly sympathetic ears
Hung on each tuneful word.

III.

Since then I've roamed the moorland wild,
With poesy and thee ;
And pressed the fragrant heather bell
With footstep light and free.

IV.

And I have known thee since, when care
And dire affliction traced
The lines that tell of weary days
No healing hath effaced.

---

*These lines were read at the Banquet given at the Queen's Hotel, Manchester, in celebration of Mr. Waugh's Seventieth Birthday.

V.

When silver crept amongst thy hair,
  Now changed to wintry rime;
And stooped thy form beneath the load
  Of unrelenting Time.

VI.

Thy lyre hath sounded 'mid the strife
  Of worldly thoughts and ways;
Thy song hath cheered the hapless wight
  With dreams of happier days.

VII.

Soon thou must lay thy harp aside,
  Hushed for the passing hour;
But memory may wake its tones
  With echoes of its power.

VIII.

The sun of thy poetic day
  For ever may have set;
But rosy are the twilight tints
  That linger round thee yet.

IX.

Ere these dissolve in darksome night,
  And leave thy soul forlorn,
May'st thou behold the breaking light
  Of an eternal morn.

BEN BRIERLEY.

SONGS OF
A Lancashire Warbler

by
Lowell Dobbs

Hoo seet mi heart gooin' back an' forrit,
Thumpin' like a facthry mule-
Then hoo spun her charms areawnd it
Like silk areawnd a spool.

£4.95

NORTHERN CLASSIC REPRINTS

The Manchester Man

(Mrs. G. Linnaeus Banks)

Re-printed from an 1896 illustrated edition — undoubtedly the finest limp-bound edition ever. Fascinating reading, includes Peterloo. Over 400 pages, wonderfully illustrated.

ISBN 1 872226 16 7 £4.95

The Manchester Rebels

(W Harrison Ainsworth)

A heady mixture of fact and fiction combined in a compelling story of the Jacobean fight for the throne of England. Manchester's involvement and the formation of the Manchester Regiment. Authentic illustrations.

ISBN 1 872226 29 9 £4.95

Hobson's Choice (the Novel)

(Harold Brighouse)

The humorous and classic moving story of Salford's favourite tale. Well worth re-discovering this enjoyable story. Illustrated edition. Not been available since 1917, never before in paperback.

ISBN 1 872226 36 1 £4.95

Poems & Songs Of Lancashire

(Edwin Waugh)

A wonderful quality reprint of a classic book by undoubtedly one of Lancashire's finest poets. First published 1859 faithfully reproduced. Easy and pleasant reading, a piece of history.

ISBN 1 872226 27 2 £4.95

Are also available in hardback at £9.95